Cambridge Vocabulary for PET

Classroom vocabulary practice

**SUE IRELAND AND
JOANNA KOSTA**

CAMBRIDGE
UNIVERSITY PRESS

University Printing House, Cambridge CB2 8BS, United Kingdom

One Liberty Plaza, 20th Floor, New York, NY 10006, USA

477 Williamstown Road, Port Melbourne, VIC 3207, Australia

314–321, 3rd Floor, Plot 3, Splendor Forum, Jasola District Centre, New Delhi – 110025, India

79 Anson Road, #06–04/06, Singapore 079906

Cambridge University Press is part of the University of Cambridge.

It furthers the University's mission by disseminating knowledge in the pursuit of education, learning and research at the highest international levels of excellence.

www.cambridge.org
Information on this title: www.cambridge.org/9780521708227

© Cambridge University Press 2008

First published 2008
Reprinted 2019

Printed in Italy by Rotolito S.p.A.

A catalogue record for this publication is available from the British Library

ISBN 978-0-521-70822-7 Edition without answers

Contents

Map of the book

Unit number	Title	Topics	Exam practice
Unit 1	Where are you from?	Countries Geography Nationalities and languages	Speaking Part 1 (Talk about yourself) Listening Part 4 (True/false questions) Speaking Part 4 (Discuss a topic)
Unit 2	How do I look?	Appearances Clothes	Reading Part 1 (Multiple choice questions) Writing Part 3 (Story)
Unit 3	Making friends	Best friends Personalities and social interaction	Reading Part 2 (Matching questions)
Unit 4	Family life	Relatives and relationships Daily life Special occasions	Listening Part 2 (Matching questions) Speaking Part 3 (Talk about a photograph)
Unit 5	In the home	Describing your home Kitchen and living room Bedroom and bathroom	Reading Part 3 (True/false questions)
Unit 6	What do you think?	The environment Opinion and attitude Feelings	Reading Part 4 (Multiple choice questions)
Unit 7	Spend, spend, spend	Shopping On the High Street	Reading Part 5 (Multiple choice questions) Speaking Part 3 (Talk abut a photograph)
Unit 8	Eating and drinking	Eating out Talking about food Cooking	Listening Part 1 (Multiple choice questions) Writing Part 3 (Informal letter)
Unit 9	Going places	Public transport Holidays	Listening Part 2 (Matching questions) Writing Part 3 (Story)
Unit 10	Having fun	Hobbies Outdoor and indoor leisure activities Party time	Speaking Part 2 (Discuss a situation) Writing Part 2 (Short message)

Unit number	Title	Topics	Exam practice
Unit 11	Education	Subjects Teaching and studying Learning a language	Reading Part 2 (Matching questions)
Unit 12	How are you?	Aches and pains Medical problems Healthy living	Reading Part 4 (Multiple choice questions)
Unit 13	Keeping fit	Sports Health and fitness	Writing Part 1 (Sentence transformation) Listening Part 3 (Fill in the spaces)
Unit 14	The natural world	Animals The countryside	Listening Part 1 (Multiple choice questions) Listening Part 3 (Fill in the spaces)
Unit 15	What's the weather like?	The weather Forecasting the weather Climates and seasons	Speaking Part 2 (Discuss a situation) Writing Part 2 (Short message)
Unit 16	The media	Television Reading books Newspapers and magazines	Reading Part 4 (Multiple choice questions)
Unit 17	Around town	Towns and cities Places and buildings Vehicles	Reading Part 1 (Multiple choice questions) Speaking Part 3 (Talk about a photograph)
Unit 18	What's on?	The arts Theatre and music Cinema	Reading Part 3 (True/false questions)
Unit 19	Technology	Communicating Computers	Listening Part 4 (True/false questions) Writing Part 1 (Sentence transformation)
Unit 20	Working life	Jobs Applying for a job Business and industry	Speaking Part 3 (Talk about a photograph) Speaking Part 4 (Discuss a photograph)

Acknowledgements

The authors would like to thank Martine Walsh, for commissioning the book, and their editors, Caroline Thiriau and Karen Jamieson, for their expert advice and guidance throughout this project. Thanks are also due to Ken and Drahos for their support and encouragement.

The author and publishers are grateful to the following reviewers for their valuable insights and suggestions:

Christine Barton, Greece
Helen Naylor, UK
Glennis Pye, Belgium
Roger Scott, UK
Mark Tondeur, UK
Valerie Walder, Switzerland
Susan Wilkinson, France

The authors and publishers acknowledge the following sources of copyright material and are grateful for the permissions granted. While every effort has been made, it has not always been possible to identify the sources of all the material used, or to trace all copyright holders. If any omissions are brought to our notice, we will be happy to include the appropriate acknowledgements on reprinting.

The publishers are grateful to the following for permission to reproduce copyright photographs and material:

Key: l = left, c = centre, r = right, t = top, b = bottom

Alamy/©40260.com for p18 (Les), /©Rubberball for p18 (Joan), /©Inmagine for p 73 (t), /©lostSense for p79; Corbis Images/©moodboard for p18 (Bella), /©Chris Carroll for p18 (Julia), /©flint for p18 (Wayne), /©Ole Graf for p73 (b), /©Vittoriano Rastelli for p91 (r); Getty Images/©First Light for p18 (Emma), /©Stone for p18 (Ken), /©Image Bank for p18 (Laura), /©Riser for p21, /©Dorling Kindersley for p54, /©Taxi for p91 (l); Kobal Collection/©Lucas Film/20th Century Fox for p82 (tr); Punchstock/©Image Source for p18 (Amy), /©Uppercut for p18 (Ed), /©Blend Images for p18 (James), /©Radius for p18 (John), /©Image Source for p18 (Ros), /©Digital Vision for p18 (Sue), /©Blend Images for p18 (Tom), /©Blend Images for p35; Rex Features for pp82 (cl) and 82 (br).

For the Listening exam practice on p.21 and p.124 based on the article 'Beer and baby sitting – a week with no women' by Andrew Argyle, *The Mail on Sunday*, 14 August 2005, © 2007 Associated Newspapers Ltd; For the material on p.57, 'Laughter is the best medicine' from 'Laughter medicine from clown doctor,' from BBC News at bbc.co.uk/news; For the article on p.75 'Sports journalist' from 'Know the real score' by Andrew Baker, *The Daily Telegraph*, 16 October 2004, © Copyright of Telegraph Media Group Limited 2007; For the article on p.83 'Making films at university' from 'Film Studies at your door,' by Simon Hogg, *The Daily Telegraph*, 9 October 2004, © Copyright of Telegraph Media Group Limited 2007; For the poem on p.86, from 'Remember when …', with the kind permission of Ahmad Anvari.

Illustrations: Robert Calow, Karen Donnelly, Mark Duffin, Sam Thompson and Kamae Design

Concept design: David Lawton

Page make-up: Kamae Design, Oxford

Picture research: Hilary Luckcock

Introduction

Who is this book for?

This book is for pre-intermediate level students working on their own who want to revise and learn vocabulary for the PET exam. Teachers can also use it in the classroom and for homework.

What is in the book?

The book contains 20 units and covers all the topics and the areas of vocabulary you need for the PET exam. There are four short tests at the end of every five units so you can check how you are getting on. At the front of the book there is an overview of the PET exam and helpful advice about learning vocabulary. At the back there are appendices with useful lists of vocabulary, extra practice and hints for the exam. There is a full key as well as sample answers for the writing and speaking activities.

What is in each unit?

Each unit is based on a topic area from the PET exam. There are three pages of activities and exercises based on that topic and the fourth page contains one or two authentic PET examination questions. There are at least two examples of each type of question in the three papers of the PET exam in this book.

What is on the audio CD?

The audio CD contains all the listening activities from each unit and any PET listening tasks from the exam practice section. There are also examples of answers to the PET speaking tasks. In the real exam you hear each recording twice so you will need to replay that track from the audio CD. Of course you can play the recordings for the other activities as many times as you like.

How shall I use the book?

You can do the units in any order and you can study on your own or with a teacher in a classroom. You will find it useful to have a notebook with you as you work through the units as some of the exercises ask you to do a short writing task. You can also use this notebook to record the new vocabulary that you learn as you go through the book. When you have finished each unit, look at the wordlist at the end of the book and use it to test yourself. Can you remember what the words mean?

Using a dictionary

Some exercises have a dictionary symbol beside them. Use the *Cambridge Learner's Dictionary*, or any other suitable English – English dictionary, to look up the meanings of the words you don't know. Write the meanings down in your notebook. The dictionary will give you plenty of useful information about the word, including its meaning, part of speech, and how it is used in a sentence. If you are not sure about the pronunciation of a word, use the CD ROM that comes with the dictionary. Click on the word and you will hear it.

How do I do the exam writing practice?

Read the question and the tip carefully. Then plan your answer. Look through the unit to see which words you can use in your answer. Look at the Writing checklist on page 97 before you begin. Remember: you **must not** pre-learn answers for the writing paper (it's easy for the examiner to spot this and you will lose marks).

How do I do the exam speaking practice?

Read the instructions and the tip carefully. Make a note of any useful words and expressions you think you may need. Look through the unit for the vocabulary you will need and at the Speaking checklist on page 96. Then do the task, either with a friend or recording yourself if you are studying alone. If there is a sample answer on the audio CD, compare your answer with this one. If not, listen to yourself and see if there is anything you could do to improve.

When should I do the tests?

There are four tests in the book, one after every five units. Each test has 30 questions based on the previous five units. After you have finished the five units do the test and then mark it to see how well you did. Highlight the questions you got wrong and go back to the units you need to look at again.

How do I learn and revise vocabulary?

Recording new vocabulary

It's a good idea to have a notebook with you when you use this book. As you work through a unit, write down the new vocabulary that you are learning. This will help you to remember it. Leave several pages for each topic so that you will have lots of space to record new words.

Put each word into an example sentence. This is especially important if a word goes with a particular preposition or can only be used with one grammatical structure.

Example
John is interested **in** football. (preposition)
I suggest **that you stay** behind to finish your work. (grammar)

Write down the translation of the word in your own language. Don't forget to include the pronunciation of the word and what part of speech it is.

Write down words which have similar meanings together.

Example
anxious, *nervous*, *worried*: you feel like this before an exam
miserable, *depressed*, *sad*: upset

Recording opposites

Recording opposites together can be helpful too, such as *boring / interesting*, *bright / dull*, *difficult / easy*.

Diagrams

Look at this spidergram from Unit 6.

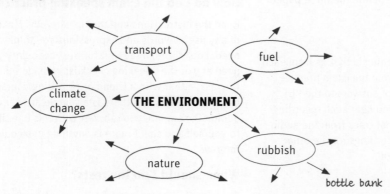

Spidergrams are useful because you can make them as big as you like in any direction. You just add more lines and more bubbles to them.

Another kind of diagram is a word tree. Add these words from Unit 20 to this word tree.

lawyer carpenter actor
salary interview office

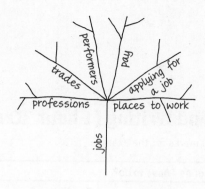

Tables

Tables are also useful for recording new vocabulary. Look at the table in Unit 15, 1.3 as an example. Tables are also very good for recording word families, as in the following example.

Noun	Person	Adjective	Verb
photograph	photographer	photographic	photograph
production	producer	productive	produce
happiness		happy	
enjoyment		enjoyable	enjoy

Labelling a drawing

Labelling a drawing or photograph is another way to record vocabulary.

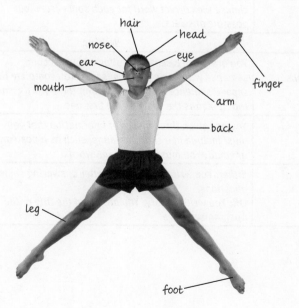

Study regularly

A final piece of advice is to try to do 10 to 15 minutes of work every day and to revise frequently. You will learn more vocabulary this way than by trying to study for a long period once a week, for example.

PET Exam Summary

Paper 1 Reading and Writing (1 hour 30 minutes)

This paper carries 50% of the total marks for the exam.

Part	What are the tasks?	What do I have to do?	Practice in this book
Reading			
1	Five multiple choice questions	You read five short texts, for example notices, emails, text messages. You choose from three possible answers to each question.	Unit 2, Unit 4, Unit 17 Exam practice
2	Five matching questions	You read five descriptions of people and eight short texts. You match the people's requirements to five of the texts.	Unit 3, Unit 11 Exam practice
3	10 true/false questions	You read a longer text and decide whether the ten statements are true or false.	Unit 5, Unit 18 Exam practice
4	Five multiple choice questions	You read a text and choose from four possible answers to each question.	Unit 6, Unit 12, Unit 16 Exam practice
5	10 multiple choice questions	There are ten spaces in a short factual text. You choose the correct word for each space from four possible answers.	Unit 7 Exam practice, Unit 8, Unit 11, Unit 16
Writing			
1	Five sentence transformations	You are given a sentence followed by a second sentence with some words missing. You complete the second sentence with no more than three words, so that it means the same as the first one.	Unit 3, Unit 13, Unit 19 Exam practice
2	Short message	You are given three pieces of information that you must include in a short message, such as a postcard or email. You must write 35–45 words.	Unit 10, Unit 15 Exam practice
3	A longer piece of writing	Either: You write an informal letter answering some questions. OR: You write a story. You are given the title or the opening sentence.	Letter: Unit 8 Exam practice Story: Units 2 and 9 Exam practice

Paper 2 Listening (30 minutes) *plus 6 minutes to write your answers on the answer sheet*

This paper has 25% of the total marks for the exam.

Part	What are the tasks?	What do I have to do?	Practice in this book
1	Seven multiple choice questions	You hear a short recording of one or two people and choose from three pictures.	Unit 8, Unit 14 Exam practice
2	Five matching questions	You hear a longer recording of a single speaker or an interview, and choose from three possible answers to the six questions.	Unit 4, Unit 9 Exam practice
3	Six spaces to fill in	You hear a longer recording and fill in six spaces in some notes.	Unit 13, Unit 14 Exam practice
4	Six true / false questions	You hear a longer informal conversation and have to decide if six statements are true or false.	Unit 1, Unit 19 Exam practice

Paper 3 Speaking

You take this test with a partner. There are two examiners – one who asks the questions and one who just listens. It takes about 10 minutes. The paper carries 25% of the marks.

Part	What do I have to do?	Practice in this book
1	The examiner asks you and your partner some questions about yourselves. (2–3 minutes)	Unit 1 Exam practice
2	The examiner describes a situation to you and gives you some pictures to help you. You discuss the situation with your partner and decide what is best. (2–3 minutes)	Unit 10, Unit 15 Exam practice
3	The examiner gives you a photograph. You have to talk about it on your own for about a minute. Then your partner will talk about a different photograph on the same topic. (3 minutes)	Unit 4, Unit 7, Unit 17 Exam practice
4	The examiner will ask you to have a conversation with your partner on the topic of the pictures in part 3. (3 minutes)	Unit 1 Exam practice, Unit 16, Unit 20 Exam practice

1 Where are you from?

Countries, geography, nationalities and languages

Countries

1.1 Look at the map of the world below and fill in the names of the continents and regions.

~~North America~~   South America   The Mediterranean
Europe   Asia   Australia   Africa   The Arctic

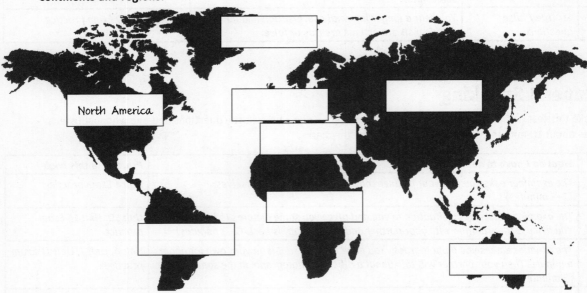

North America

1.2 Put the following countries into the correct regions in the table below.

~~The USA~~   Poland   Brazil   Kenya   China   Germany   Ecuador   Venezuela
Italy   Korea   Mexico   Egypt   Canada   India   Morocco   Zambia
Thailand   Greece   Turkey   Sweden   The Netherlands   Norway   Denmark

North America	The USA
South America	
Europe	
Asia	
Africa	

1.3 🎧 1 Listen to a couple planning a holiday. As you listen, look at the table in **1.2** and underline all the countries and regions that they mention. Then circle the region on the map that they finally choose to visit for their next holiday.

■ Geography

2.1 Look at the wordsnake and try to find the words hidden in it. Then use them to fill the spaces.

saputwaterfallaftordesertgrolitoceanterphutmountainaurthislandertyperlaw(capital)noertriverphasealosy

1 Canberra is a ....*capital*.......... city.

2 Kilimanjaro is a ....

3 Crete is an ....

4 Niagara Falls is a ....

5 The .... Nile.

6 The Black ....

7 The Sahara ....

8 The Indian ....

2.2 Complete each phrase (1–5) with the correct noun (A–E).

1 a fast-flowing A forest

2 a steep-sided B cliff

3 a beautiful, sandy C valley

4 a thick, green D bay

5 a tall, rocky E stream

2.3 Choose the correct word for each sentence.

border ~~population~~ port farmland

scenery coast soil

1 Mexico City has a ....*population*.......... of around 10 million people.

2 Many ships sail from the .... of Dover on the south coast of England.

3 Finland has a .... with Norway.

4 Scotland is famous for its beautiful lakes and mountain ....

5 A country with little .... will need to import most of its food.

6 It would be easy to grow corn in this type of ....

7 While on holiday in Turkey, we spent a day sailing along the .... in a small boat.

2.4 Choose the best word for each space (1–10).

Geography of Japan

Japan is made up of over 3,000 islands which stretch along the Pacific coast of Asia. The four largest are Honshu, Hokkaido, Kyushu and Shikoku. Japan's **(1)** ....*closest*.......... neighbours are Korea, Russia and China. Japan has many high mountains and **(2)** .... valleys and much of its soil is rocky. This means that there is a limited **(3)** .... of good farmland. Where farmland does **(4)** .... , tea, rice and fruit are grown. Because of the lack of **(5)** .... Japan's cities are mostly crowded onto the flat **(6)** .... around the coast. Japan is the **(7)** .... fishing nation in the world and shellfish and seafood are also cultivated in the **(8)** .... bays along the coast. Because of all the mountains, rivers in Japan are short and fast-flowing and so cannot be used to **(9)** .... goods. However, there is an excellent **(10)** .... of ports and harbours which are used for this purpose.

1 bordering / nearby / closest

2 low / deep / short

3 amount / number / total

4 stay / exist / live

5 area / region / space

6 ground / earth / land

7 leading / important / original

8 thin / shallow / slim

9 transport / contain / travel

10 organisation / network / company

Nationalities and languages

3.1 Use a dictionary or encyclopedia to complete the table. Add two more countries from your region of the world to the spaces at the bottom of the table, including your own if necessary.

> **V** *Vocabulary note*
>
> The names of countries, nationalities, languages and cities must begin with a capital letter:
> *Brazil, Brazilian, Portuguese and Brasilia*

3.2 Find and correct the missing capital letters in this paragraph about an author.

Frances Salter was born in the united states of America in 1957. She moved to england in 1978 with her Scottish husband, Tom. After her son Joshua was born in 1989, she started writing children's books full time. She has now published over 40 books which have been translated into 9 different languages, including french, Spanish and chinese. Frances Salter lives in london with her husband, son, and pet dog, Shanti.

Country	Adjective	Language(s)	Capital city
Canada	Canadian		
	French		
The USA			
			Warsaw
		Japanese	
			Bern
China			
			Cairo
	Mexican		
Portugal			
			Buenos Aires
		Danish	
			Madrid
Germany			
			Vienna
	Swedish		
Russia			

3.3 Complete this general knowledge crossword. All the answers are nationalities, languages or countries. Use the internet, an encyclopedia or an atlas to help you find the answers.

Across

1   This was the native language of Pablo Picasso.
5   Vaclav Havel's nationality
6   the nationality of the pop star Bono
8   This country's nearest neighbour is Sweden.
9   Nelson Mandela comes from this country.
11   the nationality of Leonardo da Vinci

Down

2   the nationality of Frederic Chopin
3   Here you can visit the ancient city of Machu Picchu.
4   This country has the largest population in the world.
7   This language is spoken in Budapest.
9   This country is in the Middle East and has a border with Turkey.
10   This is a long, thin country in Latin America.

Exam practice

SPEAKING Part 1

Think about your answers to these questions.

What country are you from?
What nationality are you?
What language(s) do you speak?
What other languages would you like to learn?
Which countries have you visited?
Which countries would you like to visit in the future?

> **Exam Tip**
>
> In this part of the test you have to talk about yourself. The questions will not be difficult so the best thing to do is relax and try to answer as fully as you can.

LISTENING Part 4

> **Exam Tip**
>
> You must listen for the feelings, attitudes and opinions of the speakers in this part of the test. Only one question in the Listening exercise on the left is NOT about the speakers' feelings – which one?
> Underline the words in the other questions which show that you have to listen for the speakers' feelings and opinions.

1 Look at the six sentences. Listen again to the conversation from **1.3** between a man, Stan, and his wife, Julie, deciding where to spend their next holiday. Decide if each sentence is correct or incorrect. If it is correct put a tick (✓) in the box under A for YES. If it is not correct put a tick (✓) in the box under B for NO.

		A YES	B NO
1	Julie thinks that holidays on cruise ships are reasonably priced.	....	....
2	Stan and Julie would like to return to some countries they have already visited.	....	....
3	Julie feels that Canada is too far away for them to visit.	....	....
4	Stan and Julie prefer to spend more time sightseeing and less time sailing.	....	....
5	Stan is disappointed with the number of activities on offer on the ship.	....	....
6	Julie will be unable to swim on this holiday.	....	....

SPEAKING Part 4

In the last part of the test the examiner will ask you to talk with your partner about a topic.
Example:
'Talk together about the places you would like to visit and what you would like to do there.'

> **Exam Tip**
>
> Talking together is rather like a game of tennis. You should take it in turns to ask and answer each other's questions.

2 How do I look?

Appearances, clothes

Appearances

1.1 Look at these pictures. Where are the people and what are they doing?

A  **B**  **C**  **D**

1.2 Use the words in the box below to describe the people in the pictures. Which word is usually only used to talk about men (write *M*)? Which ones are usually only for women (write *W*)? Which are for both (write *B*)?

good-looking	slim	tall	beautiful	handsome
smart	pretty	attractive	bald	

> ### Vocabulary note
>
> **thin**, **short**, **ugly**, **fat**
> Be careful with these words as they can sound rude. Using a negative with a positive adjective is a more polite way to say the same thing:
> *He's not very tall* (instead of *He's short*) and *She's not very pretty* (instead of *She's ugly*).

1.3 Find these in the pictures above and label the pictures.

long hair	a beard	a moustache	short hair
dark hair	fair hair	curly hair	straight hair

1.4 Use these adjectives to complete the sentences (1–5) below. One can be used twice.

light	dark	pale	bright

> ### Vocabulary note
>
> We use **light** / **dark** to describe hair.
> We use **pale** for someone's face if they are ill.

1 My hair is ....*dark*............ brown, almost black.

2 My sister's hair is .... brown, almost blonde.

3 My friend changes her hair colour every week. At the moment it's .... red.

4 I knew he was ill as soon as I saw him because his face was so ....

5 My friend's kitchen is .... yellow. I feel as if I need to wear sunglasses in there!

1.5 Put these words in order, starting with the youngest.

child	baby	teenager	pensioner	adult

1.6 Here are some sentences about a woman's life. Complete each sentence with a word or phrase from the box. Sometimes more than one answer is possible.

| middle-aged | teenage |
| youth old elderly |
| early twenties late thirties |
| fifties ~~childhood~~ young |

1 Martha had a wonderful ....*childhood*.............. growing up in the countryside.

2 She spent her .... years studying and having fun with friends.

3 She left home in her ...., worked hard and made progress in her career.

4 She got married when she was in her .... and had two children.

5 When the children were still .... she moved to the countryside.

6 Now she is a .... woman in her ....

7 Her parents are now .... so she helps them as much as she can.

8 '............................... is wonderful but being .... is not something to be afraid of', she says.

1.7 How old are you and what do you look like?
Describe yourself and some of your friends and family.
Write some sentences in your notebook.

 Vocabulary note

elderly, old
Elderly is more polite than **old** when you are describing a person.

Clothes

2.1 Look again at the pictures in **1.1**. How many of the clothes in the pictures can you name? Write a list in your notebook.

2.2 Look at the words in the box. Tick (✓) the ones that were in your list and check any you don't know in a dictionary. Which ones go with *a pair of ...*?

| blouse cap hat dress trousers jacket jeans |
| pullover shirt trainers shorts skirt suit |
| sweater T-shirt tie shoes boots pyjamas |
| coat raincoat swimming costume tracksuit |
| sweatshirt gloves |

2.3 Which of the items in **2.2** ...

1 would you wear for a job interview?
2 do you wear on your feet?
3 do you wear on your head?
4 would you wear for a party?

5 are good in cold or wet weather?
6 are good in hot weather?
7 do you sleep in?

8 are suitable for doing sport?
9 do you have in your wardrobe?
10 would a man wear with a suit?

2.4 Make at least eight phrases from the table below. Write them in your notebook. Use a dictionary to help you.

a(n) (pair of)	comfortable	silk	umbrella
	valuable	leather	uniform
	stylish	plastic	gloves
	fashionable	cotton	handbag
	tight	woollen	belt
	loose	silver	watch
	knitted	gold	tie
	old-fashioned		earrings
			tracksuit

Error warning!

cloth, clothes
Cloth is the material that clothes and other things are made out of:
The curtains are made out of heavy, blue cloth.
Clothes is the word for the things we wear:
I put my clothes on and left the house.
There is no singular word for *clothes* (we say *item of clothing*).

2.5 Look at the list of underwear. Which are for women (*W*), which for men (*M*), and which for both (*B*)?

bra   tights   stockings   socks   underpants   pants

2.6 Label the picture of the shirt with these words.

~~button~~   collar   pocket   spots   sleeves

1 ....

2 ....

3 .....button.....

5 ....

4 ....

2.7 Now complete the text below with these verbs in the correct form.

wear out   put on   fold   match   try on
fit   go with   take off

When I saw the shirt in the shop, I immediately decided to **(1)** ....try......... it ....on.......... . I loved the spotty pattern and the unusual buttons. As soon as I **(2)** .... it .... I could see that it **(3)** .... me perfectly – it was just the right size. Then the shop assistant said that the colour **(4)** .... my eyes and so, of course, I decided to buy it, even though it was expensive. I **(5)** .... it .... and changed back into my own clothes. The assistant **(6)** .... it carefully and put it into a bag for me. I'll wear it with my orange trousers. I know it will **(7)** .... really well .... them. I'm going to wear it so much, I will probably **(8)** .... it .... in a few months!

2.8 Match the definition on the left with the word on the right.

1   a kind of make-up   RING

2   this makes you smell nice   PERFUME

3   you use this to keep your nose clean   LIPSTICK

4   police officers have to wear this   UNIFORM

5   a piece of jewellery you wear on your finger   HANDKERCHIEF

2.9 ⏺ 2 Listen to four women talking about their jobs and what they wear. Number the jobs in the order you hear them.

fashion model ....   lifeguard ....   actor ....   lawyer ....

2.10 ⏺ 2 Listen again and draw lines to the correct speaker.

Who says she ...

LIFEGUARD

ACTOR

LAWYER

FASHION MODEL

1   wishes she didn't have to wear make-up every day?

2   used to wear nicer clothes in the past?

3   wears certain clothes to protect her skin?

4   doesn't really like the clothes she wears for work?

5   has to carry clothes around with her?

6   would like to wear less formal clothes sometimes?

7   has to be able to change her clothes quickly?

8   has to wear a uniform to go to work?

Exam practice

READING Part 1

- Look at the text in each question.
- What does it say?
- Choose the correct letter, A, B or C.

1

> James,
>
> I got Sue a skirt for her birthday. Why don't you get her a sweater to match it? I can show you the skirt later, if you like.
>
> Mary

Why did Mary write the note?

A She wants to know what clothes James bought Sue for her birthday.

B She is worried that the skirt she bought will not match Sue's sweater.

C She suggests that James should buy a sweater for Sue's birthday.

2

To: Jenna
From: Tara
Are you wearing your grey shirt and your silver belt to Susie's party? If not, could I wear them? I'll be very careful, I promise!

Tara sent this email because she ...

A would like to borrow some of Jenna's clothes.

B wants Jenna's advice on what to wear to Susie's party.

C wants to tell Jenna what she is wearing to Susie's party.

3

> School uniform is not necessary for tomorrow's trip but no make-up or jewellery please.

What is the purpose of this notice?

A to remind children to wear their school uniform on the trip

B to tell children what they are allowed to wear on the trip

C to explain why make-up and jewellery are not allowed on the trip

WRITING Part 3

Your English teacher has asked you to write a story. Your story must begin with the following sentence:

When the teacher walked into the room we were very surprised at his appearance.

Write your story. Write about 100 words.

 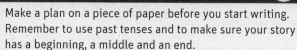

3 Making friends

Best friends, personalities and social interaction

Best friends

1.1 What makes a best friend? Complete these sentences.

- A best friend is ....
- A best friend never ....
- A best friend always ....

1.2 Look at these answers given by a group of teenagers. Underline any that are similar to your sentences in **1.1**.

A best friend is ...	A best friend never ...	A best friend always ...
someone you can tell secrets to.	talks about you behind your back.	accepts you as you are.
someone you can talk to without feeling ashamed.	tries to change you.	listens to you without complaining.
someone you can share your feelings with.	lies.	has things in common with you.
always there for you.	feels embarrassed by you.	respects you.
someone you can trust.	falls out with you.	makes you laugh when you're upset.
	gets annoyed with you.	remembers your birthday.
		helps you when you have a problem.
		keeps a promise.

1.3 Which answers in the table in **1.2** mean ...?

amusing   caring   comforting   kind   patient   reliable   understanding

1.4 *A best friend is someone you can trust* and *A best friend never lies* have similar meanings. Draw a line to join any other similar sentences in **1.2**.

1.5 Read this email and underline the words that mean ...

1   have a good relationship with
2   stop being friends with
3   become friendly again

Lucy and Jane are best friends. But last week Lucy fell out with Jane and wouldn't speak to her. Fortunately they made up again the next day and now they get on with each other even better than they did before.

1.6 Write some sentences in your notebook about your relationship with your best friend.

Personalities and social interaction

2.1 How do you think these children are feeling? Match the adjectives in the box to the children in the pictures.

> cheerful   cross   stupid
> excited   happy   interested
> nervous   shy   embarrassed
>   uncomfortable

A

B

C

D

E

2.2 🎧 3 Listen to a young man called Nick talking to his friend, Ali, about working in a children's holiday camp, and put the pictures above in order (1–5).

2.3 🎧 3 Listen again and complete these sentences with the words that you hear in the conversation.

1 Some children were rather ....*unhappy*....... at the start of the holiday because they didn't know each other. By the last day they were having such a .... time they didn't want to go home.

2 The children expected the tour of Hardwick Castle to be .... , but the guide entertained them with lots of .... stories about its history.

3 Sam felt .... the first time he went horse-riding but he soon became a .... rider even though he fell off a few times.

4 Tara jumped into the swimming pool with all her clothes on! I thought she was a .... girl. What a .... thing to do.

5 Everyone thought the party on the last evening was .... because there were fireworks and a barbecue.

2.4 Match each adjective (1–7) to its opposite (A–G).

1	fascinating	A	silly
2	cheerful	B	excited
3	sensible	C	ordinary
4	calm	D	serious
5	fantastic	E	nervous
6	funny	F	miserable
7	confident	G	dull

2.5 Now replace your answers in **2.3** with words from **2.4** that have a similar meaning.

Vocabulary note

excited, exciting
-ed adjectives describe feelings. *-ing* adjectives describe people or things:
The children were excited. They found the visit to the castle exciting.
The guide was interested in his work. That's why everyone found him interesting.

2.6 Underline the correct adjective in each sentence.

1 Nick never got *annoyed* / *annoying* with the children even though they could sometimes be *annoyed* / *annoying*.

2 Some of the fireworks in the display were *disappointed* / *disappointing* because they weren't very colourful or loud.

3 Sam is a terrible dancer. It's so *embarrassed* / *embarrassing* if he asks you to dance.

4 The journey home after the holiday was *tired* / *tiring* but we were all *excited* / *exciting* about going again next year.

2.7 Look at these pairs of words to see how adding *'ly'* to adjectives makes them into adverbs.

generous → generous**ly**   fashionable → fashionab**ly**   lazy → laz**ily**   shy → shy**ly**

Look at these pairs of sentences. Rewrite the second sentence in each so that it means the same as the first. Use no more than three words.

1 Sally always dresses in beautiful clothes.
Sally is always ....*beautifully*.... dressed.

2 James is a really hard hitter when he plays baseball.
James hits the ball .... when he plays baseball.

3 My husband is an extremely good cook.
My husband cooks extremely ....

4 Although my dog is so big he is very gentle when he plays with the cat.
My dog plays .... with the cat although he is so big.

5 The teacher told the class to be sensible.
The teacher told the class to behave ....

6 The clown did a silly dance when he came into the circus ring.
The clown came into the circus ring and danced in ....

 Vocabulary note

These adjectives don't add *ly*:
good → well
A **good** rider rides **well**.
fast → fast
A **fast** runner runs **fast**.
hard → hard
A **hard** worker works **hard**.
friendly → in a friendly way
silly → in a silly way

2.8 Make the underlined adjectives in the text below into adverbs, where necessary, to complete this letter from Matt to his friend in London.

Dear Toby,
We've been in our new home in the country for a month now. At first I was rather **(1)** <u>anxious</u> ✓ how I would get on but I've made friends **(2)** <u>easy</u> *easily*. On the first day at the new school people **(3)** <u>immediate</u> asked me to join their football game. Now they ring up **(4)** <u>regular</u> asking me to the beach or the cinema. They don't dress as **(5)** <u>fashionable</u> as in London but we can hang out together **(6)** <u>safe</u> on the streets in the evening as there's less traffic and people don't drive as **(7)** <u>fast</u> as in the city. **(8)** <u>Amazing</u>, I miss my old school **(9)** <u>terrible</u>. The teachers here expect us to work **(10)** <u>unbelievable</u> **(11)** <u>hard</u> and they speak to us very **(12)** <u>strict</u>, not **(13)** <u>friendly</u> like they did at our old school. But the lifestyle here is very **(14)** <u>relaxed</u> and we live more **(15)** <u>healthy</u> than in London as we walk or cycle everywhere and get lots of **(16)** <u>fresh</u> air. Why don't you come and stay at half term?
From Matt

Exam practice

READING Part 2

The people below all want a part-time job. Read the advertisements for eight part-time jobs. Decide which job would be the most suitable for each person.

1 Marco hopes to change his supermarket checkout job for an interesting weekend job connected with his course at art college.

2 Eddy hopes to be a professional actor and wants a part-time job that includes plenty of contact with the public. He must keep evenings and weekends free for acting with the local drama society.

3 Franca has excellent computer qualifications and experience. She wants a challenging job that she can combine with looking after her baby daughter.

4 Lydia finds restaurant and sales work boring and would love to do something unusual before she returns to university in just over a fortnight's time.

5 Alicia is at university, and her hobby is cooking. She hasn't had a job before as she is rather shy and feels uncomfortable dealing with the public. She can only work Saturdays and Sundays.

A
OFFICE ASSISTANT for afternoon work in a city-centre office, preparing bills and receipts. Computer training can be given. This job would suit a school leaver or someone wanting to get office qualifications. Childcare and canteen facilities are available.

B
HAVE YOU ever dreamed of being in the movies? Here's your chance. A major film is being made in this area and the producer needs people of all ages as extras for crowd scenes. There are no lines to learn and costumes will be provided. Hours: 8am to 8pm for up to two weeks, starting immediately.

C
Do you have a an eye for detail? Earn good money in your own home as a website designer. If you have the appropriate skills, this is an excellent opportunity to work the hours you want at home without worrying about childcare, travel or parking. Email us for further information and an online application form.

D
THE HUNTER MUSEUM
We are looking for permanent gallery assistants for Saturdays and Sundays. Ideally you will have an interest in modern painting and a helpful manner, ready to answer any questions visitors may have. You should have experience of handling money and also be able to deal with any problems that may arise.

E
Do you enjoy a chat? Why not make use of your skills by becoming a telephone sales operator? Call people and tell them about our fantastic computer products and earn extra money on any sales that you make. Weekdays and Saturdays 4pm to 9pm at our centrally-located call centre. We offer 3 and 6 month contracts.

F
A major travel firm is planning some research. We are looking for interviewers to approach shoppers and help them to complete questionnaires about their holiday preferences. This job is 10am – 4pm, weekdays only, and would suit a friendly person who enjoys meeting people.

G
ARE YOU smart, confident and outgoing? We need experienced and efficient waiters and waitresses for weddings, receptions and other important social occasions in the evenings and at weekends. You must be available at short notice.

H
WE WANT a kitchen assistant for a luxury five star restaurant, for weekends only. The duties will include preparing vegetables for lunches and dinners, making desserts and starters, and washing up. A willingness to learn is more important than previous experience.

> ### Exam Tip
>
> Read the instructions and the headlines to find out the topic. Look at the description of each person and underline what they want:
> *Marco wants <u>interesting weekend work, connected with art.</u>*
> Scan the texts. You will probably find 3 texts that are possible; C, D and G. Read them closely to match the person description and choose your answer.

4 Family life
Relatives, daily life, special occasions

Relatives

1.1 Look at the family tree
and then complete
sentences (1–10).

Joan = Ed

Ken = Sue   John   Julia = Les

Amy   Ros   Tom   Emma = James   Laura = Wayne

Bella

mother   father   son   daughter   mother in law   father in law   wife   husband
brother   sister   aunt   ~~uncle~~   cousin   niece   grandfather   grandmother
nephew   grandson   granddaughter

1 Ken is Tom's ......*uncle*......
2 Tom is Amy's ....
3 Laura is Wayne's ....
4 John is Joan's ....
5 Julia is Ros's ....
6 Emma is Sue's ....

7 Tom is Ken's ....
8 Joan is Amy's ....
9 Bella is Julia's ....
10 Ed is Les's ....

How many sets of parents are there?

Error warning!

parents, **relatives**, **relations**
Only your mother and father are your parents. All the other
members of your family are relatives or relations.

1.2 🎧 **4a** Listen to Laura, Ros and John talking about their families and complete the sentences.

A Laura has just moved ....*into*........ a new house.

Her mum looks .... Bella while she is at work.

She used to have to get .... at 5am.

She gets .... really well with her family.

Bella looks .... to being with her grandma.

B Ros wants to .... with her friends at the weekend.

Once she was .... forward to going to a party.

Her father .... her in because he thought she was too young.

Ros thinks she needs more independence as she's .... up.

c   John's grandfather .... them after his grandmother died.

John's mother had to .... him.

John and his grandfather didn't ....

Grandad .... complaining about John.

John thinks .... teenagers must be difficult.

1.3   **⊕ 4a** **Listen again to the recording. Put *L* for Laura, *R* for Ros, and *J* for John.**

Who has a good relationship with his / her parents? ......L....

Who complains about his / her father? ....

Who didn't like getting up early? ....

Who feels he / she has an unsatisfactory social life? ....

Who goes out with friends as often as possible? ....

Who thinks a parent is bringing him / her up in the wrong way? ....

1.4   **Replace the underlined words in these sentences with the correct form of the phrasal verbs in the box.**

1   Joan <u>spent her childhood</u> in Hong Kong. ......*grew up*......

2   Her mother had a nanny to help her <u>care for</u> the children. ....

3   She <u>wouldn't let them go out</u> if it was raining. ....

4   Julia and Les <u>trained</u> their three children to be kind and helpful. ....

5   When Laura <u>discovered</u> she was expecting a baby she <u>stopped</u> horse-riding. ....

6   If you can't do something at first, <u>don't stop</u> trying and you'll succeed in the end. ....

bring up	find out	give up
~~grow up~~	keep in	keep on
	look after	

1.5   **Complete the text about Amy's childhood.**

look forward to	get on with	move in with	run out of

When I was a child I used to .... going to stay with my grandparents. I loved going to the shops with Grandpa because Grandma often .... something that she needed. Later we had an extra room built onto our house and they .... us. I still .... them but it wasn't the same as when they lived on their own.

Ⓥ *Vocabulary note*

A **relationship** is the way you get on with someone. You can have a good, bad, close relationship *with* someone:
I have a very close relationship with my grandmother. I tell her all my secrets.

Daily life

2.1   **Match the two halves of the phrases.**

1	brush	breakfast / lunch / dinner
2	catch	my hair / teeth
3	eat	to school / college / work
4	get	swimming / jogging / for a run
5	go	friends
6	go	ready / dressed / undressed
7	have	home
8	leave	a bath / shower / wash
9	meet	the bus / the train

2.2   **Now make your phrases from 2.1 into sentences about what you do in the morning. Write them in your notebook.**

2.3 Look at the notes and messages on the right and answer questions 1–3..

1 Tara wants Colin to
   A finish preparing his own supper.
   B buy supper for himself and Tara.
   c have supper ready for Tara at 10:30.

> Colin!
> Can you pick up some more rice on the way home and cook it for supper? The curry's in the oven. I've eaten mine already. Back about 10:30, Tara xx

2 What is the purpose of this letter?
   A to warn parents about children going on the trip
   B to remind parents to contact the school about the trip
   c to give parents information about the school trip

> To all parents,
> School trip to Ashwell caves, 14 September.
> Please inform the school immediately if you do not wish your child to go swimming on this trip.

3 What does this card tell you?
   A full details of a future event
   B when you'll get an invitation
   c to keep a certain day free

> SAVE THE DATE!
> Sharon and Matt are getting married. 24 August.
> Invitation follows soon

Special occasions

3.1 Unscramble the words to complete the text.

Amy first met her future **(1)** (SHADBUN) _husband_, Mark, at a party. They went out together for a year and then they decided to get **(2)** (DAGEENG). Mark gave Amy a beautiful diamond **(3)** (RGIN). Six months later they got **(4)** (RADMIRE). The **(5)** (GWENDID) took place in a hotel and more than a hundred **(6)** (GUSTSE) were invited. At the reception the couple cut the **(7)** (CEAK) and Amy's father and Mark's best friend each made a **(8)** (CHEPES). A year later Amy and Mark celebrated their first **(9)** (RAYINRSAVEN) by going out to dinner.

3.2 Here are some more wedding words. Can you match these sentence halves?

1 The bridegroom   A looks after the ring on the wedding day.
2 The best man   B is the holiday the couple go on after the wedding.
3 The bridesmaid   C is the man who is getting married.
4 The honeymoon   D holds the bride's flowers during the wedding.

3.3 Add these words to the word forks below:

anniversary cake day dress guest invitation
party present reception ring speech

wedding
birthday
party

3.4 How do you celebrate special events in your family? Write some sentences in your notebook.

Exam practice

LISTENING Part 2

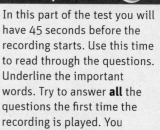 **4b** You will hear an interview with a man called Andrew, who took part in a television programme called *The week the women went*. For each question, put a tick (✓) in the correct box.

1 What was the purpose of *The week the women went*?
   A to give the women of the village a holiday together ☐
   B to find out how the men would get on without the women ☐
   C to improve the quality of life in the village ☐

2 Why didn't Andrew cook his sons' favourite food?
   A He wasn't skilled enough at cooking. ☐
   B Ready meals from the supermarket were cheaper. ☐
   C The recipes weren't in the recipe book. ☐

> ### Exam Tip
> In this part of the test you will have 45 seconds before the recording starts. Use this time to read through the questions. Underline the important words. Try to answer **all** the questions the first time the recording is played. You can check any you're not sure about the second time you hear the recording.

3 What surprised Andrew about the men's social evening?
   A that he needed a baby-sitter ☐
   B that it was so successful ☐
   C that the men didn't know each other ☐

4 Andrew and his sons found they had to
   A talk more openly together. ☐
   B go to sports events together. ☐
   C do the shopping together. ☐

5 When Kim returned she was surprised because
   A the house needed cleaning. ☐
   B the boys hadn't changed their clothes. ☐
   C Andrew had baked a cake for her. ☐

6 How has the village changed?
   A Some husbands now stay at home with the children. ☐
   B The inhabitants all work together to improve life there. ☐
   C A lot of people have moved into new houses. ☐

SPEAKING Part 3

Here is a photograph of a special occasion. The examiner will ask you to talk about what you can see in the picture.

> ### Exam Tip
> In this part of the test you have to describe a picture. You will have about 60 seconds to do this. Try to keep talking until the examiner stops you.
> Here are some useful phrases:
> *This picture shows … / It looks as if … / I think it's … because … / It makes me think of …*

5 In the home

Describing your home, kitchen and living room, bedroom and bathroom

Describing your home

1.1 Match these titles with the pictures.

block of flats / apartments   town house   country cottage

1.2 What materials do you think were used to build each of these homes? Choose from the words in the box.

steel	wood	glass
stone	brick	plastic

1.3 Look at the words in the box. Find these things in the pictures above.

hedge   fence   clothes line   garden   garage
chimney   gate   lawn   path   plants   seat
tools   steps   roof   walls   windows
balcony   entrance

1.4 ⊕ 5 Listen to a girl talking about the homes in the pictures. Answer these questions.

1 Which one did she use to live in?

2 Which one does she live in now?

3 Which one would she like to live in?

1.5 Look at these words and phrases which can be used to talk about a home.

- Circle those which complete this sentence:
  My home is …
- Underline those which complete this sentence:
  My home has …

central heating   air-conditioning   peaceful
a basement   friendly neighbours   comfortable
a flat roof   a huge garden   in a lively part of town
beautiful views   a swimming pool   lots of rooms
convenient   lots of space   neat and tidy

1.6 Now write six similar sentences in your notebook which are true of your home.

1.7 These are all rooms in a home. Check the meanings of any you don't know in your dictionary.

sitting room / living room / lounge   dining room
bathroom   toilet   basement   cellar
bedroom   hall   study / office   kitchen

Which of these rooms are in your home? Write two or three sentences, saying where these rooms are in your home. Use these words: *upstairs*, *downstairs*, *opposite*, *next to*, *at the front*, *at the back*.

1.8 Look at the list of furniture, household objects and electrical items in the box below.

Where do you keep these things in your home? Complete the table below using the words from the box. Some things may go in more than one row. Add another room in the final row if you wish.

hi-fi   CD player   DVD player   TV   ~~dishwasher~~   frying pan   computer   shaver   microwave
cooker   desk   washing machine   video recorder   table   freezer   jug   iron   corkscrew
rubbish bin   sofa   toothpaste

living room	
kitchen	dishwasher
bedroom	
dining room	
bathroom	

Kitchen and living room

2.1 Look at the picture showing some dangers in the kitchen. Complete the sentences (1–7) by choosing a word from the box below.

1 The ....handle......... of the pan should be pointing away from the room.

2 Someone could slip and fall because there is water on the ....

3 Sharp .... should be kept in a drawer, away from children.

4 The .... is too near the edge of the work surface.

5 Too many .... are plugged in here.

6 Dangerous cleaning products should be kept in a .... out of the reach of children.

7 Children's .... should not be left lying on the floor.

floor   electrical items   toys   cupboard
handle   kettle   knives

2.2 Read the descriptions (1–10) of things that can be found in the living room and write the word.

1 These are like pillows and you find them on the sofa. c _ _ _ _ _ _ _ _

2 This will give you extra light when you want to read. l _ _ _

3 You watch this when you want to relax. t _ _ _ _ _ _ _ _ _

4 This is used to display flowers indoors. v _ _ _

5 In very hot weather, one of these helps keep you cool. f _ _

6 You use this to turn electrical things on and off. s _ _ _ _ _ _

7 This is a soft, comfortable seat for one person. a _ _ _ _ _ _ _

8 This covers the floor. c _ _ _ _ _

9 Some people have these beautiful old objects in their homes. a _ _ _ _ _ _ _ _

10 These are made of cloth and hang at the windows. c _ _ _ _ _ _ _

> **(V) Vocabulary note**
>
> **Furniture** is an uncountable noun and can never be plural:
> *There is a lot of furniture in this house.*
> To talk about one thing we say *item of furniture* or *piece of furniture.*

2.3 Underline the correct word in each sentence (1–5).

1 We've decided to *move / change* house next year.

2 Now that the children have left home we don't need so much *place / space*.

3 Our new house was *designed / drawn* by a famous architect.

4 The living room has beautiful *high / tall* ceilings.

5 I don't like pale colours on walls. I prefer *bright / heavy* colours.

> **Error warning!**
>
> **place**, **space**
> **Place** is a countable noun:
> *Can you find a place to put this vase please?*
> **Space** can be used as an uncountable noun like this:
> *There isn't enough space for the vase on this shelf.*
> *There is plenty of space in the living room for the new armchair.*

Bedroom and bathroom

3.1 Match each object (1–5) with the place where you might find it (A–E).

1 rubbish bin   A on the bath

2 pillow   B covering your bed

3 tap   C in the corner of the room

4 blind   D covering the window

5 sheet   E under your head

3.2 Complete the definitions (1–8) with a word from the box. Then match the definition to the correct word (A–H).

things	warm
wash	clothes
wakes	dry
listen	look

1 This keeps you ....warm........ while you sleep.   A RADIO

2 You .... at yourself in this.   B ALARM CLOCK

3 You keep .... in this.   C TOWEL

4 This .... you up in the morning.   D BASIN

5 You put .... like books on this.   E MIRROR

6 You .... yourself with this.   F CHEST OF DRAWERS

7 You .... your hands in this.   G DUVET

8 Some people .... to this before they get up.   H SHELF

Exam practice

READING Part 3

Look at the sentences below about the ancient Chinese art of Feng Shui. Read the text to decide if each sentence is correct or incorrect. If it is correct, put A. If it is not correct, put B.

1 Feng Shui has been practised all over the world for 5000 years. ☐

2 Feng Shui says that family members will get on better with each other if the home is properly furnished. ☐

3 The entrance of the home should be neat and tidy. ☐

4 The living room should be made to look as small as possible. ☐

5 Windows in the living room should be covered. ☐

6 Stereos and CD players should be kept in the bedroom, if possible. ☐

7 A sheet could be used instead of a table-cloth to cover the TV. ☐

8 Sleeping under a window is not a good idea. ☐

9 It's important to have a good view of the bedroom door from the bed. ☐

10 A single strong light in the bedroom is better than several soft ones. ☐

> **Exam Tip**
>
> In this part of the test, the answers to the questions will come from a small part of the text only. As you do the task, underline the words or phrases that gave you the answer to each question.

Feng Shui

Feng Shui is the art of arranging your home and the things in it in the best possible way. It began in China about 5000 years ago, but recently architects and designers all over the world have started to include the idea in their work. The most important thing to understand about Feng Shui is the idea of chi, which means vital energy or life force. The art of Feng Shui is to make sure that the right objects are in the right places so that the chi can flow freely around the home. This is said to create good health and financial well-being as well as improved relationships between parents and children and husband and wife. You can improve your own Feng Shui by trying some of the techniques listed below.

Firstly, keep the hall of your home clear of shoes, umbrellas and other objects. This is to allow the chi to enter your home freely. If possible, put a small indoor fountain in this part of your home.

In the living room, choose furniture which is the right size for the room and arrange it so that people can move around the room comfortably. If the room is small, hang a mirror to create a feeling of space. Make sure you have blinds or curtains to prevent the chi from escaping.

The bedroom is considered a very important area in Feng Shui. It is best not to have a television or any other electrical item in here, but if you find it impossible to live without them, you can cover them with a plastic table-cloth when you have finished using them. The table-cloth must be plastic – other materials will not work. It is also important to unplug everything before you sleep. The head of the bed should be against a wall rather than under a window, as this would allow your chi to escape. You should be able to see the door easily while you are lying in bed. Place lamps by your bed for lighting instead of bright lights in the ceiling.

Try these simple ideas for a few months and see how much energy and happiness you can bring into your home.

Test One (Units 1–5)

Choose the correct letter A, B, or C.

1   Which of the following is NOT a country?
    A Germany   **B** Polish   **C** France

2   Europe, Africa and Asia are all ....
    A continents   **B** countries   **C** capitals

3   A little .... runs through the garden of my parents' house.
    A sea   **B** river   **C** stream

4   The .... of the United Kingdom is about 60 million.
    A population   **B** region   **C** border

5   We went sailing on the sea during our holiday and stopped for lunch at a little ....
    A coast   **B** cliff   **C** bay

6   A .... is a very dry place where few plants can survive.
    A valley   **B** forest   **C** desert

7   My brother was not a very good-looking child, but now he's an adult, he's very ....
    A pretty   **B** beautiful   **C** handsome

8   People always say they love my .... hair but I would prefer it to be straight.
    A long   **B** blonde   **C** curly

9   You are looking very .... today. Are you feeling OK?
    A pale   **B** light   **C** fair

10 These .... are too tight! I'll have to lose some weight!
    A trainers   **B** trousers   **C** pockets

11 Do you think this blouse .... with this jacket?
    A matches   **B** fits   **C** goes

12 My trainers are old and .... out but I still love them.
    A worn   **B** put   **C** taken

13 A person who never lies is someone you can ....
    A promise   **B** trust   **C** remember

14 If I tell you a .... you mustn't tell it to anyone else.
    A secret   **B** story   **C** message

15 Sam was .... when he fell off the horse.
   A annoying   **B** embarrassing   **C** embarrassed

16 Max is very ....; I hope he can afford such expensive gifts.
   A reliable   **B** generous   **C** confident

17 Maria got very .... with Harry when he refused to put his toys away.
   A nervous   **B** uncomfortable   **C** cross

18 Jess .... with Sophie because she didn't go to the party.
   A fell out   **B** got on   **C** made up

19 I'm so excited! My sister's just had a baby girl and I've always wanted a ....
   A cousin   **B** granddaughter   **C** niece

20 Many children are .... by a single parent.
   A grown up   **B** brought up   **C** given up

21 After breakfast Josh .... ready for school.
   A got   **B** did   **C** made

22 Sharon and Matt are having a party to .... their wedding anniversary.
   A celebrate   **B** invite   **C** remember

23 The bridegroom's voice was shaking when he stood up and ....
   A cut the cake   **B** put on the ring   **C** made a speech

24 All the wedding .... brought presents.
   A relatives   **B** guests   **C** visitors

25 I like my home because there is a lot of .... for all my things.
   A space   **B** place   **C** area

26 Which of these is NOT a room in a house?
   A basement   **B** cooker   **C** hall

27 Could you pull down the .... please? The light is shining in my eyes.
   A window   **B** curtains   **C** blind

28 Don't touch the .... of the saucepan, it may be hot.
   A drawer   **B** handle   **C** iron

29 Which of the following would you NOT expect to find on a bed?
   A sheet   **B** pillow   **C** carpet

30 Which of the following is always found in a bathroom?
   A tool   **B** tap   **C** toy

6 What do you think?

The environment, opinion and attitude, feelings

The environment

1.1 Look at the spidergram on the right and think of words to add to it.

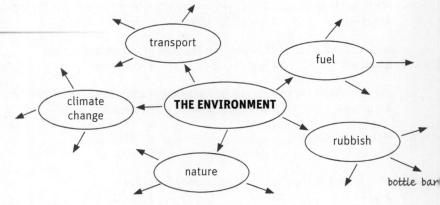

1.2 Look at the words and phrases in the box below. Check any you don't know in a dictionary and then add them to the spidergram. Some words may go in more than one place.

~~bottle bank~~   petrol   litter   pollution   traffic jams
cardboard   rainforests   tins   plastic   paper
floods   plants   cans   storms   public transport
coal   glass   global warming   packaging
wildlife   metal   electricity   waste   recycle
oil   the countryside

1.3 Use some words or phrases from the spidergram to complete this text.

> **Vocabulary note**
>
> **nature, the environment, the countryside**
> Look at how we use these words:
> *We should all work hard to protect the **environment**.* (the air, land and water where people, animals and plants live.)
> *My son is very interested in studying **nature**.* (the natural world: plants, animals, oceans. Do not use an article here!)
> *I love going for long walks in the **countryside**.* (land where there are farms, fields and forests, and no towns or cities.)

A Planet in Trouble

There are more problems facing the environment today than at any time in the past. World population stands at around 6 billion and by the end of the 21st century, it may reach 8 or 10 billion. To satisfy the needs of these people, we are destroying **(1)** ....*rainforests*.... and other natural places so that we can grow food and put up buildings. This creates **(2)** .... of the land, sea and air, which can be very bad for the health of humans and **(3)** .... such as birds and animals.

Most scientists now agree that it has also caused **(4)** .... and this means that the temperature of the Earth is rising. The ice at the North Pole could melt, raising sea levels and causing serious **(5)** ....

Generally, the Earth's weather will be worse and there will be more wind, rain and **(6)** .... However, there are things we can do. Scientists are working to come up with ways of making power that do not cause so much pollution. People at home can recycle their **(7)** .... paper and glass and try to use less **(8)** .... by turning off lights, TVs and stereos when they are not using them. We could all use our cars less and walk or use **(9)** .... more.

Opinion and attitude

2.1 Look at the text in **1.3** again. What is the writer's purpose in the text? Tick (✓) two of the following:

1 to **advise** people on the best way to recycle their waste. ....

2 to **describe** some difficulties in the environment. ....

3 to **explain** the reasons for some problems in the environment. ....

4 to **discuss** different ways of producing energy. ....

5 to **suggest** ways that governments can help the environment. ....

2.2 Now look at the texts below and say what the writer's purpose is in each case. Circle the best verb for each.

1 If you want to help local insects and birds, a really good way to do it is to let your garden grow a little bit wild and not tidy it up too much. If you don't want the whole garden to be untidy, just choose one area at the back of the garden and let nature take control of it.

> suggest
> remind
> review

2 From the mid 1800s until the 1950s large cities in Britain, such as London and Manchester, suffered every winter from thick, yellow fog. It was caused by smoke from burning coal in homes and factories. Many people became ill from it every year. Eventually the government passed laws to control the amount of fuel that could be burnt in the cities and the fog disappeared.

> persuade
> explain
> warn

3 There are several ways that you can use less power in your home. First of all, if you are cold, put on a jumper instead of turning up the heating. If you are hot, turn down the heating rather than opening a window. Switch the TV off when you are not using it and always buy low-energy light bulbs.

> recommend
> promise
> compare

2.3 ⊕ 6 Listen to five short conversations. For each one choose <u>one</u> word from the box to describe the speaker's main purpose. Write it on the line.

Conversation 1: ....

Conversation 2: ....

Conversation 3: ....

Conversation 4: ....

Conversation 5: ....

> encourage   persuade   recommend   decide   advise
> promise   agree   disagree   remind   complain

2.4 Use the words below to talk or write about your opinions on the environment.

I believe ...
I think ...
I don't think ...
In my opinion ...
According to ...
I feel ...
I'm confident that ...
I'm sure ...
I wish ...

ⓥ Vocabulary note

We say *I don't think it's a good idea to burn rubbish* NOT *I think it's not a good idea to burn rubbish*.

To give someone else's opinion you say *According to (Professor Turner)* ...

To give your own opinion you say *In my opinion* NOT *According to me* ...

Feelings

3.1 All the words in the box below describe feelings. Which are positive and which are negative? Write *P* or *N* beside each word. If you think the word is neither positive nor negative, put a circle around it.

depressed ...N...   amazed ....   annoyed ....   ashamed ....   delighted ....
disappointed ....   frightened ....   relaxed ....   satisfied ....   worried ....

3.2 Match each word in the box below with a word with a similar meaning in the box above.

angry   upset   embarrassed   anxious
surprised   afraid   miserable   very happy
calm   pleased

Error warning!

Nervous is another word for **worried** and **anxious**:
I felt very nervous before my exam.
Nervous does not mean angry.

3.3 How would you feel in these situations (1–8)? Use words from **3.1** and **3.2**.

1 You have a very important job interview later today. ....

2 You have just found out that you failed your driving test. ....

3 You have just spilt coffee on your friend's new white carpet. ....

4 Your friend has just spilt coffee on your new white carpet. ....

5 You have heard that your aunt has just had a baby. ....

6 You have just finished painting a beautiful picture. ....

7 You are in the middle of a wonderful holiday by the sea. ....

8 You have had a new haircut and everyone is saying how good you look. ....

3.4 Talk or write about yourself. Look at the words in the lists in **3.1** and **3.2**. What makes (or made) you *happy*, *anxious*, *frightened*, *nervous* etc.?

Example:
I feel happy when I listen to my favourite music.
I felt embarrassed and nervous when I had to speak in public at my brother's wedding.

3.5 Use one of the following verbs in the correct form to complete the sentences. More than one choice may be possible.

to love   to like   to hate   to be keen on   to dislike   to mind   ~~to be fond of~~   to look forward to

1 My grandfather is a lovely man and I ...am fond of... him.

2 I can cook if I have to, but I don't really .... it.

3 My son .... football. It's his favourite sport.

4 I don't .... walking, but I prefer to drive if I have the choice.

5 There are not many people I .... but my horrible history teacher is one of them.

6 They .... each other very much so they are going to get married.

7 I .... it when people drop litter on the floor – it's so unnecessary.

8 I'm going on holiday next week and I am .... it so much. I can't wait!

Exam practice

READING Part 4

Read the text and questions below. For each question, choose the correct answer, A, B, C or D.

Bird watching in Colombia

Luis Morales is 18 years old and comes from a tiny village in the Andes mountains in Colombia. Until about seven years ago, one of Luis's favourite activities was to go into the thick forest surrounding his home to hunt and kill the wildlife, especially birds. Now, however, he and a group of other local youths work with an international organisation called Wildlife World, to study and protect the birds and their environment.

Wildlife World has set up several of these groups across the area. 'Information we get from the children helps us learn how the birds and other animals use the forest, what they eat and how best we can protect them. The project has worked very well and we hope to set up more groups in the future,' says area leader Felipe Ramos.

Luis is the oldest and most experienced member of his group, having been a member since he was just 11. 'Before I joined, I planned to leave the village as soon as I was old enough to go and find work in the city, like most young people do,' Luis says. 'But now I want to go to university, become a scientist and return here to carry on working to save these rare birds and their environment. Being part of the group has had a huge effect on me.'

Luis also spends time with the younger children in the village. 'There is not much to do here after school,' he says, 'so I try to involve them in our activities. As well as bird watching and nature studies we also do drama and art. The drama has been particularly successful and we now have a theatre group of 30 children, which tours in the area, performing different plays.'

1 In this text the writer is …
  A describing village life in Colombia.
  B suggesting ways to help the environment.
  C giving information about a project.
  D advising children to join Wildlife World.

> **Exam Tip!**
>
> Some questions in this part of the exam will test your understanding of the whole text. Now circle the questions that test your understanding of attitude and opinion.

2 Seven years ago, what was Luis's attitude towards birds in the forest?
  A He wanted to learn more about them.
  B He knew they were rare and in danger.
  C He thought it was fun to destroy them.
  D He was not interested in them at all.

3 How does Luis feel about the group?
  A He is happy because he is leaving it soon.
  B He is grateful because it has changed his life.
  C He is miserable because he wants to stay longer.
  D He is worried because he wants more young people to join.

4 According to Felipe Ramos, what is the purpose of the group?
  A to find out about the behaviour of local wildlife
  B to teach children how to look after the environment
  C to protect children from wild animals in the forest
  D to collect information about how people use the forest

5 What would Felipe Ramos say about Luis?

A Luis is a wonderful person and he knows so much about the birds and animals in this forest. He is also a really great musician.

B Luis has just joined us and is already very important to the group, mainly because he is so good with the younger children.

C I'm going to miss Luis when he goes away to study. But I am delighted that he will be back afterwards to continue his work here.

D When I first met Luis he was preparing to move to the city to find work. Luckily, I persuaded him to stay and join my group. He never wants to leave.

7 Spend, spend, spend

Shopping, on the High Street

Shopping

1.1 🔘 **7a** Listen to three people, Dario, Margot and Jennie, talking to an interviewer about going shopping. What has each person bought today?

	dress
	jacket
Dario:	earrings
	jumper
	book
Margot:	skirt
	handbag
	CDs
Jennie:	magazines
	hat
	shoes

1.2 🔘 **7a** Listen to the interviews again.

Which person …

1 already has a job?

2 thinks he or she is a sensible shopper?

3 gets cash to spend from his or her parents?

4 dislikes going shopping?

5 looks at the computer before going out?

6 sometimes regrets buying things?

7 is looking forward to having a credit card?

> ### Ⓥ *Vocabulary note*
>
> **pay**, **charge**
> To **pay** (verb) someone is to give them money.
> To **charge** (verb) someone is to ask them for money.
> A **charge** (noun) is the amount of money you pay:
> *I had to pay a small charge for having my glasses mended. The garage only charged me for the tyre. I didn't have to pay anything for having it fitted.*

1.3 📖 Use a dictionary to check these words about paying and then put them in the sentences.

bill	cash	charge	cheque	exchange	deposit	discount	receipt	refund	reduced

1 I'm afraid I haven't got enough .... with me. Do you mind if I pay by .... ?

2 A: When I tried this sweater on at home it was too tight. Could I have a .... ?

   B: Certainly, if you've still got your ....

3 If you show your student card at the cash desk you'll get a 10% ....

4 I'm afraid there's a small .... for fitting this watch battery.

5 These shoes are too big. I'd like to .... them for smaller size.

6 We can order this computer for you but you'll have to pay a .... for it.

7 We'll send you a .... for the full amount. Please pay it within 7 days.

8 I never pay the full price for anything. I always wait until it's .... at the end of the season.

1.4 How often do you go shopping? Where do you go? What sort of things do you like to buy? How do you pay for them? Write some sentences in your notebook.

On the High Street

2.1 Complete the words. Where could you go ...

1 to find out the cost of a letter to Italy? p _ _ _ o _ _ _ _ _ _

2 to get your winter coat cleaned? d _ c _ _ _ _ _'s

3 for some shampoo and soap? c _ _ _ _ _ _'s

4 for a cut and blow-dry? h _ _ _ _ _ _ _ _ _ _'s

5 to book a holiday? t _ _ _ _ _ a _ _ _ _'s

6 to have a photo of your family taken? p _ _ _ _ _ _ _ _ _ _ _ _'s

7 to have a new watch battery fitted? t _ _ _ _ _ _'s

8 for some fast food to take home? t _ _ _ _ _ _

9 to collect your medicine? p _ _ _ _ _ _

10 to buy a variety of different things? d _ _ _ _ _ _ _ _ _ _ s _ _ _ _

2.2 Look at the store guide below and check any words you do not know in a dictionary. Put the name of the department in each gap.

STORE GUIDE

Babyclothes	1	Electrical appliances	LG	Lighting	2	Sewing goods	G
Bed and bath linen	2	Floor coverings	2	Lost property	2	Sports equipment	LG
Bedroom furniture	2	Flower shop	G	Luggage	G	Sunglasses	G
Beds	2	Furniture	2	Menswear	LG	Swimwear	1
Boys' clothes	LG	Garden furniture	LG	Mirrors and pictures	2	Toilets	1
Cameras	2	Gift wrapping service	G	Nightclothes	1	Toys	LG
Clocks	1	Girls' clothes	2	Parents' room	2	Watches	G
Computers and telephones	2	Hats	2	Perfumes and make-up	G		
Cooking equipment	2	Information desk	G	Pharmacy	G		
		Jewellery	G	Public telephones	2	G=Ground floor	
Customer service	LG	Ladies' fashions	1	Radios and televisions	1	LG=Lower ground floor	

A shopping trip

I went to the department store to buy a present for my cousin's new baby girl. I found some lovely little soft pink woolly socks in the **(0)** ..Babyclothes.. department on the first floor. Then I went down to **(1)** .... where I bought a pretty little cloth rabbit. I had it wrapped at the **(2)** .... That was right by the **(3)** .... so I got some green plastic buttons and a packet of needles to mend my coat with. I also needed a few things for my new flat – pillowcases and towels from the **(4)** .... department, a large stainless-steel saucepan from **(5)** .... and a small carpet from the **(6)** .... section. I looked at a beautiful red Italian leather suitcase in the **(7)** .... department but I couldn't afford it. Instead I got a lovely gold chain from the **(8)** .... section.

By now I had a headache so I got some aspirins from the **(9)** .... On my way out I remembered it was my grandmother's birthday so I got her a dozen bright yellow roses in the **(10)** .... I'd got lots to carry and I'd spent a lot of money but at least I shan't have to go shopping again for a while!

2.3 Notice the order of these adjectives:

I found some lovely little soft pink woolly socks.

Can you find five more combinations of adjectives and nouns in 2.2 and add them to the table?

	opinion	size / age / shape / feel	colour	material	noun
some	*lovely*	*little soft*	*pink*	*woolly*	*socks*

2.4 **Now complete these sentences. Using all these adjectives in the correct order.**

1 There's a .... shop at the corner of our street. (*little / fascinating / antique*)

2 One day I saw a .... spoon in the window. (*silver / old / beautiful*)

3 It was next to a .... statue. (*painted / wooden / large*)

4 I looked in my .... purse and found I could just afford to buy it. (*leather / new / green*)

5 I bought the spoon and the shopkeeper packed it in a .... box. (*cardboard / small / white*)

2.5 **Find the answers to the puzzle.**

1 This moving staircase will take you to the upper or lower floors.

2 This means the item has been made cheaper.

3 goods that have been arranged for people to look at

4 Keep this because you might want to exchange what you've bought.

5 The assistant will do this to the things you have bought.

6 This person is in charge of the whole store.

7 notes and coins

8 This is how much you must pay for something.

9 You go here to pay when you've finished shopping for food.

10 His job is to persuade you to buy things.

11 When you go to a store this is what you are.

Exam practice

READING Part 5

Read the text below and choose the correct word for each space.

THE FUTURE OF SHOPPING

Travel agents, mobile phone stores and banks may soon completely **(0)** ....A......... from the High Street as people **(1)** .... more and more goods online. **(2)** .... to a recent report, increasing **(3)** ....of shoppers are using the internet for their holidays, CDs, books, mobile phones and banking. **(4)** .... customer service and reasonable delivery **(5)** .... mean that many people nowadays do much of their shopping from in front of their computer screens. **(6)** .... it seems that customers still prefer to buy clothes and items such as shoes, bags and jewellery from high street stores and shopping centres, where they can look around and **(7)** .... things on before handing over **(8)** .... money.

0	**A**	disappear	**B**	escape	**C**	leave	**D**	pass
1	**A**	book	**B**	apply	**C**	require	**D**	order
2	**A**	According	**B**	Due	**C**	Up	**D**	Further
3	**A**	crowds	**B**	quantities	**C**	numbers	**D**	groups
4	**A**	Sure	**B**	Complete	**C**	Safe	**D**	Efficient
5	**A**	amounts	**B**	sums	**C**	charges	**D**	prices
6	**A**	Therefore	**B**	Whatever	**C**	Somewhere	**D**	However
7	**A**	keep	**B**	take	**C**	try	**D**	leave
8	**A**	her	**B**	our	**C**	your	**D**	their

> **Exam Tip**
>
> Before you start, read the text right through and try to understand the general meaning. After you have finished the questions, read it through again to check that your answers make sense.

SPEAKING Part 3

In this part of the test the examiner will give you a photograph and ask you to talk on your own about it.

> **Exam Tip**
>
> Don't worry if you don't know the word for something – try and explain it in another way using phrases like:
> *I'm not sure what it's called in English but you use it for ... / It's like ... / You can find it in ...*

7b Look at the photograph. It shows someone in a shop. Talk about what you can see in the photograph. You could record yourself talking about the picture, then listen to Rosa describing it. Are there any things you talked about that she doesn't mention? The table is called a *counter* – how does Rosa describe it?

8 Eating and drinking

Eating out, talking about food, cooking

Eating out

1.1 Look at the menu and match each heading below to the correct section.

1 Desserts .....   3 Main courses .....

2 Drinks .....   4 Starters .....

1.2 Decide what each of these friends might choose to eat.

1 Sarah hasn't eaten all day and is cold and hungry. She loves red meat and wants a full three-course meal to help her get warm again.

   ....

2 Liz just wants a snack so she'll have a starter and something sweet to finish with. She can't eat any fish or milk products.

   ....

3 Ross is a vegetarian and also avoids fish and pasta. He's supposed to be on a diet so he won't have a starter. However he'd like a nice sweet dessert.

   ....

4 Tim always chooses something different from his friends. He's looking forward to a big meal that includes fish, meat, vegetables and something tasty to finish.

   ....

   How about you? What would you choose for yourself from this menu?

MENU

A.................. (ALL SERVED WITH A ROLL AND BUTTER)
FRENCH ONION SOUP
MELON WITH HAM
SEAFOOD SALAD

B.................. (ALL WITH SALAD OR COOKED VEGETABLES
AND YOUR CHOICE OF POTATOES)
STEAK WITH ONIONS AND PEPPER SAUCE
PAN-FRIED COD WITH PEAS
CHICKEN AND MUSHROOM PIE
ITALIAN SPAGHETTI WITH TOMATO SAUCE
JACKET POTATO FILLED WITH CHEESE, HAM OR
BAKED BEANS

C.................. (SERVED WITH VANILLA ICE CREAM)

CHOCOLATE CHEESE CAKE
HOT APPLE PIE WITH REAL BUTTER PASTRY
FRUIT SALAD

CHEESE AND BISCUITS

D..................
MINERAL WATER (STILL OR FIZZY)
SOFT DRINKS (COKE, LEMONADE ETC.)
ICED TEA OR COFFEE
FRUIT JUICE (ORANGE, GRAPE ETC.)
POT OF TEA OR COFFEE

Talking about food

2.1 Which adjectives from the box can be used to describe the food (1–6)? Sometimes more than one adjective is possible.

1 chocolate cheesecake ....

2 vindaloo curry ....

3 strawberry ice-cream ....

4 unsweetened lemon juice ....

5 pear and apple tart ....

6 unripe apples ....

cold
bitter
hot
rich
sour
sweet

2.2 **Make adjectives from these nouns and then complete sentences (1–6) below:**

| cream | fish | fruit | juice | salt | taste |

Vocabulary note

We can add –*y* to some nouns to make an adjective:
salt → salty
juice → juicy
Notice what happens when the noun ends in *e*.

1 Let's buy some of these oranges; they look really ....

2 This soup tastes quite .... There must be some seafood in it.

3 I'm afraid the potatoes were too .... Are you feeling thirsty as well?

4 I'd love another slice of pizza. It's very ....

5 Mix the flour with the eggs and milk until it is nice and ....

6 This drink is supposed to be made from fresh melon and bananas but it doesn't taste very .... to me.

2.3 **Look at this list of food.**

biscuits	bread	cake	cabbage	cereal
chicken	chips	coffee	coke	fish	fruit
honey	jam	pasta	pie	pizza	tea	toast

Which of the items can you refer to using ... ?

1	*a bowl of*	cereal
2	*a slice of*	
3	*a loaf of*	
4	*a mug of*	
5	*a spoonful of*	
6	*a can of*	
7	*a packet of*	
8	*a piece of*	

Vocabulary note

slice, piece
A **slice** is a **piece** of something that has been cut with a knife.

2.4 **Look at the groups of words (1–9) below. Which is the odd one out? Why?**

1	knife	mug	chopsticks	spoon
2	turkey	duck	chicken	lamb
3	roll	cake	pizza	toast
4	tea	cocoa	coke	coffee
5	plate	pan	saucer	dish
6	grapes	cabbage	spinach	peas
7	frozen	bitter	sweet	sour
8	microwave	kettle	barbecue	oven
9	burger	French fries	hot dog	omelette

2.5 **Here are three interesting expressions. Notice the food word in each expression.**

It's not really my *cup of tea*.	(I don't really like it.)
They are *full of beans*.	(They're very lively.)
It was a *piece of cake*.	(It was very easy.)

Can you put the correct expression into each sentence (1–3) below?

1 I don't know why I worried about the exam; it was a ....

2 Heavy metal music really isn't ....

3 Even after they'd spent the afternoon playing football, the children were still ....

Cooking

3.1 Do you enjoy cooking? Here is a recipe for some biscuits. They are healthy, easy to make and they taste really good. Put the instructions for the biscuit recipe (A–F) in the correct order. The first one has been done for you.

Breakfast cookies

Ingredients
350 grams unsweetened breakfast
    cereal (e.g. porridge)
200 grams brown flour
135 grams raisins
35 millilitres milk
2 eggs
2 large spoonfuls of honey

Instructions
A Roll it out like pastry and cut it into interesting shapes. ....
B Before you start, turn the oven on to 220°. ...1...
C When the biscuits are cool, share them with your friends. Enjoy! ....
D When it is nice and smooth stir in the cereal and raisins and leave it in the fridge for about half an hour. ....
E Place the shapes in a baking tin and bake them in the oven for 12–15 minutes. ....
F Put the flour into a bowl and pour in the honey, eggs and milk and mix everything together well with a spoon. ....

3.2 Look at the recipe again and underline any verbs connected with cooking.

3.3 Complete sentences (1–6) below, using the correct form of the words in the box.

boil   mix   grill
roast   bake   stir
fry

1 You can .... sausages in a pan or .... them on a barbecue.

2 Bread must be .... in a hot oven or it won't rise properly.

3 A traditional British Sunday lunch is a large piece of meat .... in the oven with vegetables.

4 The easiest way to cook an egg is to .... it in a pan of water.

5 It's best to use a wooden spoon to .... food while it's cooking.

6 You can .... all the ingredients for your cake in this big bowl.

3.4 Write some instructions for making a cup of tea. You may need some of these words: add, boil, cup, kettle, lemon, milk, pot, pour, sugar, tea, water

3.5 Choose the best word for each gap (1–10).

> ### Vocabulary note
> You can add *–ful* to a noun to show an amount: *a spoonful of sugar, two cupfuls of flour, a mouthful of food.*

Not just about food

Cookery classes teach young people a range of useful **(1)** .... , not just how to prepare meals for friends and family. Cooks have to think **(2)** .... : after all it's no good making a cake and **(3)** .... it into a cold oven. Then it's essential to **(4)** .... the recipe carefully. Stirring 50 grams of salt into your cake instead of five grams will certainly **(5)** .... it!
There are many dangers in the kitchen – sharp **(6)** .... , hot cookers and **(7)** .... kettles for example. Knowing what to do if there is an accident will be very useful in the world outside the kitchen. But the greatest pleasure comes from turning raw **(8)** .... into a dish that **(9)** .... far better than anything from the supermarket or fast food van, and is certainly much **(10)** ....

1 instructions / skills / views
2 ahead / forwards / straight
3 baking / putting / roasting
4 attend / notice / follow
5 injure / spoil / damage

6 glasses / knives / tins
7 heating / boiling / cooking
8 parts / ingredients / objects
9 tastes / enjoys / pleases
10 stronger / fitter / healthier

>
> ### Vocabulary note
> Notice how we can use the verb **to taste**:
> *These potatoes taste too salty. (are)*
> *Always taste your food before you add any salt to it. (try / test)*

Exam practice

LISTENING Part 1

 8 **For each question there are three pictures and a short recording. Choose the correct picture and put a tick (✓) in the box below it.**

1 What does the man choose for dessert?

A ☐ B ☐ C ☐

2 What does the woman's rice dish contain?

A ☐ B ☐ C ☐

3 What will Sam's mother do on his birthday?

A ☐ B ☐ C ☐

WRITING Part 3

This is part of a letter you receive from an English penfriend.

> I hope you enjoy making this biscuit recipe. Tell me about the food in your country. Do you have a big breakfast? What's your favourite meal?

Now write a letter, answering your penfriend's questions. Write about 100 words.

Exam Tip

To get a good mark for this part, remember to answer all the questions in your penfriend's letter! Start and finish your letter in a suitable way and sign it.

9 Going places

Public transport, holidays

Public transport

1.1 Match the ways of travelling with the vehicles in the box.

bike	car	plane	train	boat
	bus	helicopter	ship	

by air: ....*plane*........   by rail: ....

by land: ....   by road: ....

by sea: ....

1.2 Describe your favourite and least favourite ways of travelling using the adjectives in the box below and any ideas of your own.

I like / don't like travelling by .... because it is ....

fast / slow   reliable / unreliable
safe / dangerous   noisy / quiet
cheap / expensive   crowded / empty
comfortable / uncomfortable
convenient / inconvenient

Ⓥ *Vocabulary note*

Travel, **journey**, **trip**, or **voyage**?
Travel is the verb:
I love to travel. / I have travelled a long way today.
Journey is a noun used to talk about travelling from one place to another:
I had a terrible journey to work this morning. / The baby fell asleep during the journey.
We use **trip** when we go away somewhere, usually for a short time, and then return:
I went on a trip to the seaside. / My father is away on a business trip.
A **voyage** is a long journey by sea.
We had a very calm voyage across the Atlantic when we went to New York.

1.3 Where would you expect to see these notices? Match the notices (A–H) to the places in the box.

car park   airport   train   aeroplane   road   bus

A **Do not leave anything valuable in your vehicle.**

B **Please fasten your seatbelt.**

C Do not lean out of the window.

D **Please do not leave any baggage unattended.**

E **Do not speak to the driver**

F **Keep to the right at all times.**

G **Your life jacket is under your seat.**

H **Please give up this seat if an elderly person needs it.**

1.4 Divide the words in the box into three groups: travelling by RAIL (*R*), travelling by AIR (*A*), or BOTH (*B*).

flight   passenger   security   airport   platform   boarding pass   destination   station   luggage
gate   waiting room   driver   duty-free   terminal   baggage collection   flight attendant   delay
lost property   arrivals   departure lounge   check-in   airline   timetable   pilot   fare

1.5 Which word from **1.4** do you associate with each of the following (1–10)?

1 checking when the next train goes ......*timetable*......

2 getting an umbrella back ....

3 waiting for your suitcase ....

4 buying perfume and watches ....

5 the price of your ticket ....

6 waiting to board the plane ....

7 passing the time at a train station ....

8 getting your cases weighed ....

9 having your bag checked ....

10 asking for a drink on a plane ....

1.6 Mark these words and phrases *B* (before flying), *O* (on the plane), or *A* (after the flight).

do some duty-free shopping ...*B*...
arrive at the airport ....
board the aeroplane ....
land ....
find the correct check-in desk ....
collect your baggage ....
go to the correct gate ....

go through customs ....
go through security ....
go through immigration ....
take off ....
watch a safety demonstration ....
fasten your seatbelt ....
leave the airport ....
check in ....

1.7 (⊕ 9a) Listen to two announcements, A and B, and answer these questions by circling the best answer in each case.

1 Announcement A is at a railway station / an airport.

2 Announcement B is at a railway station / an airport.

3 Both announcements are about special offers / changes to services.

1.8 (⊕ 9a) Listen again and fill each gap with one or two words.

Announcement A	Announcement B
There are delays because some stations do not have enough **(1)** ......*staff*...... .	*Flight 397 to Budapest has been cancelled because of the* **(1)** ....
Passengers can find information by looking at the **(2)** .... *around the station.*	*The first flight to Budapest in the morning is at* **(2)** ....
Delays could be as long as **(3)** .... *minutes.*	*Passengers cannot leave the* **(3)** .... *until they have given their details.*
If you go to the ticket office, you will be able to get a **(4)** .... *on your ticket.*	*The airline will pay for all food and* **(4)** ....

Holidays

2.1 People go on holiday for lots of different reasons. Do you go on holiday for any of these reasons? Underline the reasons in the box below that apply to you and circle the ones that don't.

> to rest and relax   to meet people and make friends   to have fun   to learn about new cultures   to see lots of different places   to do sport and get fit   to explore distant parts of the world   to learn a foreign language   to learn a new skill   to try new food

2.2 Match one or two of the reasons in **2.1** to each different type of holiday below.

> camping   backpacking   beach   cycling   touring   adventure   skiing   sailing   sightseeing   painting   cooking   walking

2.3 Here is a list of the different kinds of places you can stay when you are on holiday. Underline your favourites.

> campsite   hostel   guesthouse   inn   bed and breakfast   hotel

2.4 Look at the words in the box and match them to the places to stay in **2.3**.

> luxury   tent   room service   single room   souvenir shop   sports facilities   shared bathroom

2.5 Add *-er*, *-or*, or *-ist* to make people out of these words.

> cycle   drive   backpack   climb   hitchhike   camp   travel   tour   translate   interpret   reception

2.6 Read the text below and decide where it comes from.
Think about the writer's purpose in writing the text. Choose from the following words.

> brochure   letter   magazine article   encyclopedia   guide book

If you are looking for a relaxing **(1)** .... away from the stresses of your everyday life, then you could not choose a better hotel than Preston Manor. The hotel is set in the most beautiful gardens you can imagine and every room has delightful **(2)** .... of the surrounding countryside. A wide range of **(3)** .... activities is available to our **(4)** .... , including indoor and outdoor swimming, tennis, golf and snooker. Other **(5)** .... include a mini gym, two fantastic restaurants, a hairdresser and a bar. From the moment you arrive to the moment you **(6)** .... at the end of your stay, we will look after your every need. To **(7)** .... a table in the restaurant or to **(8)** .... a room for an **(9)** .... stay, just call, on 020 7465 9387. We look forward to being of service.

2.7 Now fill each gap in the text in **2.6** with a word from the box below.

> break   leisure   overnight   views   guests   reserve   book   facilities   check out

Error warning!

We use **stay** and not **live** when we go to hotels or other places for a short visit:
I live in Manchester, but I'm staying with my aunt for the school holidays. / We stayed in a fantastic hotel when we were on holiday in Spain last year.

2.8 Talk or write in your notebook about holidays you have been on. Where did you go, what kind of accommodation did you stay in, how did you get there, and what did you do when you were there?

Exam practice

LISTENING Part 2

🔊 9b **You will hear a man talking on the radio about a hotel. For each question choose the best answer, A, B or C.**

1 The Icehotel at Jukkasjarvi
   A has to be rebuilt every year.
   B is perfect for all types of guest.
   C is a long distance from the nearest airport.

2 According to the speaker, the village of Jukkasjarvi
   A is a good place to go out in the evenings.
   B has limited opportunities for sightseeing.
   C has very good facilities for tourists.

3 People visiting the hotel need to know that
   A there will be no ice sculptures this year.
   B bookings cannot be made for December.
   C the hotel will not be finished until mid January.

4 Guests who wish to do the ice-sculpture class
   A can choose what time they want to do it.
   B must be able to speak English or Swedish.
   C do not need to bring anything with them.

5 The speaker warns listeners that the trips offered by the hotel are
   A very popular.
   B fairly dangerous.
   C rather expensive.

6 The speaker says that heated accommodation
   A is reserved for those who need it most.
   B is preferable to the ice rooms.
   C is available if you choose to use it.

WRITING Part 3

Your English teacher has asked you to write a story. Your story must have the following title:

An amazing journey

Write your story. Write about 100 words.

10 Having fun
Hobbies, outdoor and indoor leisure activities, party time

Hobbies

1.1 What hobbies have you and your friends and family got? Make a list.

1.2 Look at this spidergram.

Add these hobbies to it.

cooking, ~~coins~~, cycling, dolls, electric guitar, football, horse-riding, gymnastics, ~~jogging~~, keep fit, knitting, models, painting, photography, sculpture, sewing, skiing, stamps, violin

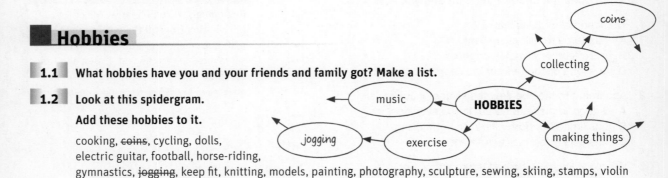

Now add the words from your list in **1.1** if they are not already there.

1.3 Which of the above hobbies are these people talking about?

1 Personally I think you can get some great effects with film but most people use digital nowadays.

2 It's a great way to enjoy the scenery but it's annoying if you get a flat tyre and have to repair it by the roadside.

3 Dad's made a special display stand for my collection – I've got national costumes from 25 different countries.

4 You have to be very strong and have excellent balance, especially when you're performing on the bar.

5 It's not just about going out for nice rides in the countryside. Feeding and cleaning are very hard work.

6 Working with water-colours is quite difficult because you can't hide your mistakes like you can with oils.

7 It's best to turn on the oven and weigh everything out first before you start mixing any ingredients together.

8 My parents complain about the noise so I usually practise with headphones on, unless they've gone out.

9 My uncle travels to lots of different countries and brings back all the new issues for me to stick in my book.

10 I've got plenty of wool and the needles are quite big so I'm hoping to finish this sweater by the weekend.

1.4 Complete the text with the correct form of these verbs.

add	arrange	build	buy	exchange	forget	increase	join	prevent	stick

Collecting things

Most people collect something in their lives. It might be a collection of family photos **(1)** ......stuck........ into an album or holiday souvenirs **(2)** .... on a shelf. Other people **(3)** .... up collections for a particular purpose: paintings that will **(4)** .... in value, for example, or memories recorded on tape to **(5)** .... a changing way of life from being **(6)** ....

Some people collect everyday items that are easily available, such as football programmes or teaspoons. Other collections, like old tools, wooden elephants or old-fashioned dolls, are more specialised. Collectors **(7)** .... to their collections in different ways: by **(8)** .... things on the internet or from antique shops or flea markets. Others **(9)** .... clubs where they can **(10)** .... items with one another.

1.5 Find words in 1.4 that mean:

1 a book that you keep a collection in. ....

2 something you buy to remind you of a holiday or special event. ....

3 a place, usually out of doors, selling used and second hand goods. ....

1.6 Have you ever collected anything? Where did you get the items for your collection? Where is your collection now? Write some sentences in your notebook about your collection.

Outdoor and indoor leisure activities

2.1 ⏺ 10a Look at the pictures below. You will hear four people talking about what they do in their free time. Match the speakers to the pictures.

A   B   C   D

Speaker 1 ....   Speaker 2 ....   Speaker 3 ....   Speaker 4 ....

2.2 Use the words in the box to complete these compound nouns and adjectives from the recording:

jacket	minute	camp	water	wear	week	wet

1 what you wear on your feet   foot <u>w e a r</u>

2 Saturday and Sunday   _ _ _ _ end

3 a field to put tents in   _ _ _ _ site

4 lasting half an hour (adj)   30-_ _ _ _ _ _

5 keeps you dry (adj)   _ _ _ _ _ proof

6 a suit to protect you in the water   _ _ _ suit

7 it will save your life if you fall in the sea   life _ _ _ _ _ _

       ⏺ 10a Listen again to check your answers.

Error warning!

camping / **campsite** and **parking** / **car park**
Camping and **parking** are activities; **campsite** and **car park** are places:
We went camping last summer. The campsite had a big car park so there wasn't any problem about parking.

2.3 (10a) Listen again. What clothes and equipment do the speakers need for their activity? Make notes.

Speaker 1: Equipment _tent_ ....
Clothes ....

Speaker 2: Equipment ....
Clothes ....

Speaker 3: Clothes ....

Speaker 4: Equipment ....
Clothes ....

2.4 Use these words to complete the letter about joining a club.

secretary	fee	individual	cards	discount	joining
advice	facilities	benefits	registration form	clothing	membership

Dear Ben,
Have you considered taking out (*1*) ..membership.. of the Lakeland Rock Climbing Club?
(*2*) .... include use of the Club (*3*) ...., loan of maps and equipment and expert
(*4*) .... Members also get money off a range of goods at a number of shops supplying outdoor
(*5*) .... when they show their membership (*6*) ....
(*7*) .... has never been easier with (*8*) .... membership at £15.95 and a reduced
(*9*) .... of £9.95 for students. If you pay by bank transfer you receive a 10% (*10*) ....
Just fill out the (*11*) .... at the bottom of this letter.
We look forward to welcoming you at the Lakeland Rock Climbing Club soon.
Yours sincerely,
Rod Marsh (Club (*12*) ....)

Arranging a party

3.1 Match the verbs (1–10) and nouns (A–J).
There may be more than one possible answer.

1	book	A	the neighbours
2	buy	B	all night long
3	clean up	C	the barbecue
4	cook	D	yourselves
5	decide on	E	some drinks and snacks
6	light	F	the food
7	warn	G	invitations
8	send out	H	a band
9	enjoy	I	a date
10	dance	J	the next day

3.2 Put your answers in the order in which you would do them. There may be more than one possible answer.

1	decide on a date
2	
3	
4	
5	
6	
7	
8	
9	
10	

3.3 Use your answers to **3.2** to write a paragraph describing a party you helped to organise.

Exam practice

SPEAKING Part 2

> **Exam Tip**
>
> This part of the test should be a discussion so you should talk with your partner. Use phrases like: *What do you think about ...? / What about ...?, / I think this would be good because ... / That's a good idea but ...*

 10b Your friend has moved to a new town and wants to make some new friends. **Talk about the different things your friend can do to meet people and say which you think is best.**

Now listen to two students doing this part of the exam and compare your answer to theirs. Do you agree or disagree with the speakers?

WRITING Part 2

You have joined a club and you think your friend would like it too. Write an email to your friend.

In your email you should:
• say what club you have joined
• tell your friend where and when it meets
• explain why you think your friend would like it.

Write 35–45 words.

> **Exam Tip**
>
> There will be three points in your answer to this part. Try to avoid repeating words from the question in your answer and don't add any unnecessary information that will make your answer too long.

Test Two (Units 6–10)

Choose the correct letter A, B or C.

1   The children were asked to pick up the .... in the school playground.
   A waste   **B** litter   **C** pollution

2   Which of the following is NOT a type of fuel?
   A petrol   **B** coal   **C** electricity

3   We used to live in the city, but we much prefer it here in the ....
   A countryside   **B** nature   **C** environment

4   If you are telling someone the reason why something happened, you are ....
   A persuading   **B** warning   **C** explaining

5   If your friend is giving you some ideas on how to use less electricity, she is ....
   A advising   **B** comparing   **C** reviewing

6   I was a bit .... with my test results – I will have to work harder next time!
   A worried   **B** nervous   **C** disappointed

7   How much will you .... to repair these shoes?
   A cost   **B** charge   **C** pay

8   The hairdryer broke the first time I used it so the store gave me a full ....
   A receipt   **B** discount   **C** refund

9   You'll find pillows in the .... department.
   A bed and bath linen   **B** nightclothes   **C** floor covering

10 The menswear department sells ....
   A purses and handbags   **B** shirts and ties   **C** skirts and blouses

11 The salesman was wearing a ....
   A smart new green woollen jacket.   **B** woollen green new smart jacket.   **C** green smart woollen new jacket.

12 If you are not satisfied with the service in this store ask to speak to the ....
   A customer   **B** travel agent   **C** manager

13 I don't really like strong, black, coffee. I find the taste too ....
   A sour   **B** hot   **C** bitter

14 Can I offer you a .... of chocolate cake to have with your tea?
   A slice   **B** loaf   **C** spoonful

15 Before you begin cooking, ... the oven on to 220 degrees.
   A keep   **B** turn   **C** get

16 One way to cook potatoes is to .... them in a pan of water with a little salt.
   A bake   **B** fry   **C** boil

17 Before you begin cooking, it's a good idea to get all your .... ready.
   A pieces   **B** ingredients   **C** parts

18 Beat the mixture until it is .... and creamy.
   A smooth   **B** flat   **C** low

19 I find it more .... to use my car when I go grocery shopping, but I always use the bus to get to work.
   A reliable   **B** convenient   **C** dangerous

20 We had a great holiday, but the .... home was terrible. It took 6 hours to travel 100 km!
   A trip   **B** way   **C** journey

21 It took us a long time to get through all the .... checks at the airport.
   A security   **B** terminal   **C** destination

22 After the plane has .... off I can relax and start to enjoy the flight.
   A gone   **B** flown   **C** taken

23 Which of the following CANNOT be an occupation?
   A interpreter   **B** backpacker   **C** driver

24 The hotel has wonderful ...., including three restaurants and a 25 m swimming pool.
   A facilities   **B** bookings   **C** brochures

25 Students for the .... class will need to bring their own paper and brushes.
   A photography   **B** drawing   **C** painting

26 Would you like to see my .... of old postcards?
   A demonstration **B** collection   **C** performance

27 If you're going sailing you'll need a .... in case you fall in the water.
   A raincoat   **B** helmet   **C** life-jacket

28 It was impossible to find a .... so we had to leave the car in the street.
   A parking   **B** park   **C** car park

29 I'm thinking of joining the local cycling club but .... is quite expensive.
   A membership   **B** fee   **C** benefit

30 We had .... our neighbours about the party but they still complained about the noise.
   A invited   **B** warned   **C** apologised

11 Education

Subjects, teaching and studying, learning a language

Subjects

1.1 Complete this puzzle with the names of some subjects and activities you can study at school, university or college.

1 You often do this subject in a laboratory.

2 The answers to clues 1, 4 and 21 are examples of this.

3 They speak this language in France.

4 This is the study of living things.

5 In this subject you read and discuss novels, poetry and plays.

6 This is a short way to say the answer to clue 13.

7 In this subject you learn how to act.

8 In this subject you learn about the past.

9 In this subject you learn about instruments and you can learn to play one.

10 This is the study of money and the financial world.

11 They speak this language in Mexico.

12 This is the study of painting and drawing.

13 In this subject you work with numbers.

14 In this subject you learn how to prepare food.

15 In this activity you run, jump and throw.

16 This is the name of the language you are practising now.

17 This is the study of the world and all the countries.

18 In this subject you might learn Chinese, Polish, German, Russian or Spanish etc.

19 In this subject you might play football, hockey, basketball or volleyball etc.

20 In this subject you learn how to use a camera.

21 This is the study of heat, light and movement etc.

1.2 Write your own definition for *Information Technology*. ....

1.3 Say or write down your favourite and least favourite subjects at school.

....

1.4 Look at these words. Which of them have similar meanings? Which are opposites?

pointless   useful   useless   enjoyable
interesting   boring   hard   easy   difficult
important   dull

1.5 Use the words in **1.4** to complete the following sentence so it is true for you.

I think .... is a / an ....
subject because ....

Teaching and studying

2.1 Where do these people give classes? Match people from the first box with places from the second box.

professor   teacher   lecturer   instructor   trainer

primary school   secondary school   university
college   driving school   sports club

2.2 What are the most important qualities in a teacher? Decide which of these is the *most* important and which is the *least* important in your opinion.

strict   funny   kind   serious   clever   fair
intelligent   patient   reasonable   punctual

Error warning!

fun / funny
Fun is a noun and means *enjoyment*:
I had a lot of fun in Mr Gillam's history lesson today.
Funny is an adjective and means *amusing*.
Mrs Bailey is very funny. Her jokes always make me laugh.

2.3 Look at the phrases in the box below. Underline the ones which complete sentence 1, and circle the ones which complete sentence 2. You can circle and underline the same phrase if necessary.

1   A good teacher (is)   2   A good student (is) ....

gets good grades   a good listener   good at explaining things   works hard   uses modern methods
uses traditional methods   makes good progress   concerned about the welfare of the students
always marks homework on time   gives a lot of homework   doesn't give much homework
pays attention in class   doesn't talk much   talks a lot   hands homework in on time

2.4 Which sentences from **2.3** do you agree with?

2.5 Talk or write about the best teacher(s) that you have now or you had in the past.

2.6 Look at the groups of words (1–10) below. Which is the odd one out? Why?

1 learn	study	revise	pass
2 college	grade	school	university
3 class	lesson	course	primary
4 exam	degree	diploma	certificate
5 advanced	elementary	difficult	intermediate
6 library	laboratory	classroom	equipment
7 pupil	professor	student	learner
8 board	bell	desk	break
9 text book	dictionary	novel	translate
10 composition	essay	homework	report

Vocabulary note

to pass an exam / to take an exam
Look at these sentences:
I am going to take the PET exam in June.
I really hope I pass! If I don't pass, I will take the exam again in November.

2.7 🔘 **11** Listen to a woman talking about her school days and answer the questions below.

1 Which of the following were important at the woman's school? Circle as many as necessary.
being correctly dressed / being punctual / being polite / passing exams

2 What did the woman do to make the teacher angry?
she was absent from school / she did not do her homework / she was talking in class

3 What punishment did the teacher give the woman? He made her ...
stay behind after school / pick up litter in the playground / write 100 lines

2.8 What are or were some of your school rules? How do or did teachers punish pupils?

2.9 Have you ever been on a school trip? Did you enjoy it and what did you learn? Read this information about school trips from a website. Choose the best word for each space.

School Trips to Chocolate World

Bringing children to Chocolate World is not only fun, it is also good for their **(1)** .... Our organised school trips are carefully planned to support many areas of the primary school **(2)** .... , including history, geography and technology. Children will learn all sorts of interesting **(3)** .... about cocoa, the plant whose bean is the main ingredient of chocolate. They will **(4)** .... where and how it is grown, how it was used in the past, and why it is still so important today. They will also be **(5)** .... how chocolate is made and will be able to see the machines working in our factory. To **(6)** .... fully from the trip we suggest teachers also book a talk **(7)** .... can be given on a variety of topics to suit the needs and interests of the group. Included in the price of the trip are worksheets for students to complete as they go around the exhibition. Teachers **(8)** .... older students are welcome to create their own worksheets. For more information, or to make a booking, please call 020 8891 7630.

1	instruction / education / training	5	learnt / studied / shown
2	course / curriculum / subject	6	benefit / achieve / understand
3	facts / news / truths	7	what / who / which
4	discover / find / tell	8	bringing / carrying / getting

Learning a language

3.1 What do you find easiest and most difficult about learning English? Choose from the box.

> grammar   spelling   pronunciation
> vocabulary   reading   writing   speaking

3.2 Why are you learning English? Choose as many reasons as you like from the following box.

> to get a qualification   to pass an exam
> for personal interest   for pleasure   for work

3.3 Complete each sentence with the correct word.

1 Could you *translate* / *interpret* this paragraph into English please?

2 I'm sorry, I can't read your handwriting. What does this word *say* / *mean*?

3 Can anyone tell me the *meaning* / *understanding* of 'shiver'?

4 How do you *pronounce* / *spell* 'accommodation'? Does it have one *m* or two?

Exam practice

READING Part 2

The people below all want to do a part-time course. Underneath are descriptions of 8 part-time courses. Decide which course would be most suitable for each person.

1   Luis was given a digital camera for his birthday and would like to learn how to use it. He is a beginner and he wants to do the course for fun rather than for a qualification.

2   Gloria studied art at university but has not painted for many years. She is free during the day. She is interested in painting pictures of nature but does not need a qualification.

3   Julia would like to improve her computer skills. She already has some basic knowledge but needs a certificate for her new job. She can study evenings and weekends.

4 Kim wants a course where she can learn how to become an author. She works in the morning but is free every afternoon. She is keen to do lots of homework.

5 Claude is very interested in modern literature, and would like to learn more about it. He would like to get a qualification if possible. He works in the evening so can only do classes during the day.

PART-TIME COURSES AT BURLEY COLLEGE

A On this course we will look at several different art forms, including painting, digital photography, and printing. The course leads to a diploma in art, and every student will be expected to take the exam. The course is only suitable for those who have studied these art forms before. It is on Mondays at 10am.

B Do you dream of one day writing your own novel? If so, then this could be the course for you. We will look at how to create believable characters, interesting story lines and beautiful language. You will have to be prepared to do a lot of writing at home, and listen to other people criticise it! Classes are from 2pm to 5pm, Fridays.

C If you already have some skill and knowledge of art, but are simply out of practice, then this could be the course for you. We will start slowly but by the end of the course classes could be quite challenging so it will not be suitable for beginners. Classes will take place on Thursday mornings and we will be working outdoors in the countryside most of the time.

D This course explores the poetry and novels of 10 living authors. We will read and discuss the books and then you will be given compositions to write for homework. We will be working towards an examination, and those who pass will get a certificate at the end of the course. The course takes place on Wednesdays at 3pm.

E Employers these days require basic computer skills and if you don't have them you are at a big disadvantage compared to other job hunters. This course is only suitable for complete beginners, but with the certificate you get at the end, you should be able to get a good job. The course is on Tuesdays and Thursdays at midday.

F This course is on Saturdays at 1pm. It covers the basics of digital photography. You will learn how to take fabulous pictures which will impress all your friends with the minimum of effort. There is no exam to revise for at the end, and the only homework will be to take lots of pictures, so you can just relax and enjoy the course.

G This course will examine the literature of past centuries and look at whether the work is still important in today's modern world. There will be a lot of homework on this course, mainly reading but also writing essays, so you will have to be prepared for that. The course takes place on Thursday afternoons at 2pm.

H Our new computer course is suitable for those who have used a computer before but now need to increase their knowledge. It takes place on Wednesdays at 6.30pm. There is an examination at the end and if you pass you will be able to show the qualification to your employer, as it is widely recognised in the business world.

Exam Tip

There will be two or more texts which look as if they could be right when you first read them. The correct one will have ALL the information asked for.

12 How are you?

Aches and pains, medical problems, healthy living

a

b

c

d

e

f

g

h

i

j

k

Aches and pains

1.1 Look at the picture and label the parts of the body.

1.2 Here are some more parts of the body. Check the meanings in your dictionary.

ankle	chin	knee	nail	neck	finger	back
shoulder	skin	throat	thumb	toes	tooth

1.3 🔊 12 Listen to three people talking to their doctor. Write down in your notebook the parts of the body you hear mentioned.

1.4 Match the adjectives (1–5) to the nouns (a–e).

I've got a

1 sore   a cough
2 broken   b temperature
3 nasty   c throat
4 runny   d leg
5 high   e nose

> **Ⓥ Vocabulary note**
>
> These are the five aches:
> *I've got backache / earache / a headache / toothache / (a) stomach ache*
> Which ache always has *a* in front of it?

1.5 Can you make these words about injuries and illnesses? You heard some of them in the conversations in **1.3**.

1	Tablets, pills or a liquid – this will help you get better.	ICEDMIEN	m _ _ _ _ _ _ _
2	You stick this on a cut to keep it clean.	SPARLET	_ _ _ _ _ _ _
3	You put this on a wound to protect it.	REDSINGS	_ _ _ _ _ _ _ _
4	A nurse or doctor might tie this round your injury.	BEGANAD	_ _ _ _ _ _ _
5	This vehicle takes you to hospital.	NEBULAMAC	_ _ _ _ _ _ _ _ _
6	The doctor gives you this to take to the chemist.	PINCERSIRTOP	_ _ _ _ _ _ _ _ _ _ _ _
7	This is the time you see the doctor or dentist.	PANTMENTPIO	_ _ _ _ _ _ _ _ _ _ _

1.6 *One* of the three verbs in each sentence is *incorrect*. Cross out the incorrect verb.

1 Sally didn't *look / feel / ~~get~~* very well during the exam.
2 I usually *take / catch / get* at least one cold during the winter.
3 Don't *cut / hurt / damage* yourself on that broken glass!
4 This medicine *looks / tastes / feels* horrible.
5 Fortunately no-one was *damaged / hurt / injured* in the accident.
6 James *broke / hurt / pulled* his leg when he was skiing.

> **Ⓥ Vocabulary note**
>
> **hurt**, **injure**, **damage**
> **Hurt** and **injure** are used with people and animals, and **damage** is used with things:
> *The falling tree damaged the car roof but luckily the driver wasn't hurt / injured.*

1.7 Complete this note from a college student to his teacher.

Dear Miss Scott,

I'm afraid I can't come to school because I'm not very (1) .... well .... I caught a (2) ....
last week and now I've got a nasty (3) .... , a sore (4) .... and a high (5) ....
as well. I went to see the (6) .... and she told me to (7) .... at home for a few days.
She gave me a (8) .... for some (9) .... I had to get it from the (10) .... It
doesn't (11) .... very nice but I hope it will make me feel (12) .... soon.

Pierre

1.8 What about you? Write your answers to these questions.

When did you last catch a cold? How did you cure it?   Have you ever broken a bone? How did you do it?

Which do you think is worse – toothache or a headache? Why?

Medical problems

2.1 🎧 **12** Listen again. What do the doctors tell their patients?

Patient	Problem	The doctor says ...
A		
B		
C		

2.2 Your friend has some medical problems. Look at your replies below. What did your friend say to you?

1 You should put a plaster on it.

2 Why don't you phone the dentist for an appointment?

3 You'd better get some cough medicine.

4 What about getting some new glasses?

5 Don't come near me; I don't want to catch it!

2.3 Underline the words in **2.2** that introduce advice or suggestions.

> **Vocabulary note**
>
> **You'd better ... / Why don't you ... /**
> **You should ...** are followed by the infinitive:
> *You'd better go to the doctor. / Why don't you go to bed?*
> **What / How about ... ?** takes the –ing form
> *What about going to the doctor?*

2.4 Your friend is worried. What might you say?

1	*I've put on a lot of weight and all my clothes are too tight.*	*You'd better ....*
2	*I spend all my money on fast food.*	*You should ....*
3	*I can't sleep at night.*	*Why don't you .... ?*
4	*I'm bored at weekends.*	*What about .... ?*

Healthy living

3.1 Read these rules for a healthy lifestyle. Which of them do you follow?

1 Aim to eat five pieces of fruit or vegetables a day.
2 Be active in your everyday life.
3 Eat regular, healthy meals.
4 Get fit in your leisure time.

5 Eat less fatty food.
6 Eat regular, sensible snacks.
7 Drink plenty of water.

3.2 Now match the rules to the sentences below.

A ......6......

It's OK to eat between meals, but choose food that will fill you up, like cereal bars, fruit and nuts, rather than chips, biscuits and chocolate.

B ....

When you're thirsty, your brain can't work properly. Plenty of water, juice, low fat milk or fruit tea will help you to concentrate, but avoid too much strong coffee and alcohol.

C ....

Having three balanced meals each day is the best way to make sure your body gets everything it needs. Don't miss breakfast – it gives you a good start to the day.

D ....

Why not use the stairs instead of the lift, or walk or cycle to work, or get off the bus a stop early and walk the rest of the way?

E ....

Most of us don't eat enough of them – but they are essential for good health. Remember, a can of tomatoes or a glass of fresh fruit juice also counts as one piece.

F ....

Watching TV or playing computer games for too long means being inactive – dance, or walk or cycle to the gym in the evenings and at weekends. You'll feel fitter and healthier.

G ....

Grill or bake food, rather than frying it, and don't add too much cream and butter to cooking. But remember you do need some healthy fats like sunflower oil and olive oil in your diet.

3.3 Read through the rules again and fill in the lists below:

Healthy	Unhealthy
cereal bars, fruit, nuts	chips, chocolate

3.4 Which rule in **3.1** do you consider the most important? Have you got any other suggestions for a healthy lifestyle? Write them in your notebook.

Exam practice

READING Part 4

- **Read the text and questions below.**
- **For each question, mark the correct letter, A, B, C or D.**

Laughter is the best medicine

Every week, Dr Doppit goes round the wards at the children's hospital. But instead of a white coat and a stethoscope, Dr Doppit has a red nose and carries balloons. She is the hospital's 'clown doctor' and her real name is Hilary Day.

After studying drama at university, Hilary saw an advert for a clown doctor at the hospital. 'The job was perfect for me,' she says. 'My mother and grandmother were both nurses, so caring for people is in my blood. Also, I love doing children's theatre.'

Before she started, Hilary did four weeks training, where she learnt how to do magic tricks and make balloons into funny shapes. She also had to study child psychology and basic medicine.

Her visits to the hospital start with a meeting with the nursing staff to find out which patients a visit will be most useful for. Most children are delighted to see a clown, but there are some who are too ill, or are afraid of clowns. Hilary always checks first. Then she does some magic, makes balloon animals or tells them a story.

'We know that laughing can have a positive effect on a person's health,' says Hilary. 'It produces chemicals in the brain that make you relax and feel better.' Everyone agrees that regular visits from Dr Doppit can make a big difference to a child's recovery. 'Children in hospital miss their everyday life at home and at school,' says one hospital manager. 'As well as possibly being frightened and homesick they are often bored. The clown doctor gives them something to look forward to and happy memories to take home afterwards.'

---

1 What is the writer's aim in this text?
- **A** to describe a typical day in a children's hospital
- **B** to explain a method of helping young patients
- **C** to encourage doctors to learn some circus skills
- **D** to show students how to get a job in a hospital

2 Why was Hilary particularly suitable for the job of clown doctor?
- **A** She had studied medicine at university.
- **B** She already knew how do magic.
- **C** She enjoyed working with children.
- **D** She had been a nurse in a hospital.

3 Before Hilary starts, the staff tell her which children ...
- **A** have asked to see her.
- **B** are going to leave the hospital soon.
- **C** want to hear a particular story.
- **D** will benefit most from her visit.

4 The hospital manager thinks that Dr Doppit's visits ...
- **A** are useful if the parents can't visit.
- **B** help the children get better more quickly.
- **C** might be frightening for some children.
- **D** help the children forget their stay in hospital.

5 What might a child say about Dr Doppit?
- **A** 'Dr Doppit visited me today – she took my temperature and listened to my chest and then she told the nurses to give me some different medicine.'
- **B** 'I didn't like the clown with the balloons who came to my bed to see me, she was frightening – I hid under the covers until she'd gone.'
- **C** 'Dr Doppit comes every day. Everybody thinks she's funny but sometimes the nurses tell her to go away because laughing's not good for us.'
- **D** 'I feel ever so much better – this really funny clown told me a story and did some magic. I couldn't stop laughing. I hope she comes again before I go home.'

13 Keeping fit

Sports, health and fitness

Sports

1.1 Look at the pictures. What sports can you see? Write the name of each sport in the first column and the equipment you need in the second. Some have been filled in to help you.

	Sport	Equipment
1		*weights*
2	*tennis*	*balls and racket*
3		
4		
5		
6		
7		
8		*gymnastic rings*
9		
10		*fishing rod*
11		*boxing gloves*
12		

1.2 Look at the list of sports from **1.1**. Do we use *play*, *go* or *do* with each one?

play	*go*	*do*
tennis	*skiing*	*gymnastics*

1.3 Now add these words to the table in **1.2**: *athletics, running, swimming, volleyball, horse-riding*

 Vocabulary note

play / go / come / do
We use **play** with a game:
The students like to play football in the lunch break.
We use **go** with the –*ing* form of the verb when we are talking about a sporting activity:
We went sailing on Saturday.
When someone joins us in a sporting activity we use **come** and the –*ing* form:
Sally came sailing with us at the weekend.
We use **do** with nouns for physical activities like ballet and judo:
I do judo on a Wednesday and ballet every Saturday.

1.4 Complete this text with the correct form of *play, go, come* or *do*.

I'm preparing to run in a marathon – that's a 40 kilometer road race. I **(1)** .... jogging every morning and **(2)** .... swimming twice a week. I **(3)** .... for a run most evenings and at weekends. I sometimes ask my son to **(4)** .... with me but he prefers to **(5)** .... horse-riding. My daughter **(6)** .... ballet at the sports centre and while she is at her class I **(7)** .... weight-lifting in the gym. I **(8)** .... to basketball practice regularly because I'm in the team and we **(9)** .... matches most weekends. In my lunch hour I often **(10)** .... squash with a colleague. By **(11)** .... so much exercise I hope to be really fit for the marathon. I'm not going to relax afterwards either – I plan to **(12)** .... skiing with my family in the Swiss Alps!

1.5 How much do you know about sports? Choose the right answer.

1 You play golf on a golf
  A track.
  B course.
  C park.

2 To score in hockey you hit the ball
  A into the net.
  B over a bar.
  C through a basket.

3 A game ends in a draw when
  A a player is injured.
  B both sides have the same score.
  C one team gives up.

4 You score goals in
  A table tennis.
  B squash.
  C ice hockey.

1.6 Which one is the odd one out? Why?

Example   long jump   diving   high jump   100 metres
***Diving** is a watersports event, the others are athletics*

1	coach	champion	winner	partner
2	track	pool	changing room	court
3	sailing	snowboarding	waterskiing	windsurfing
4	match	competition	result	game
5	tennis	volleyball	table tennis	basketball

 Error warning

practise, **practice**
Remember that to **practise** a sport means to do training for a sport. Sports **practice** is the time when you do training:
I have swimming practice on Wednesdays.
I am not very good at back stroke so I really have to practise that more.
Practice is the noun. Practise is the verb.

1.7 What sports do people do at school in your country? Which do you prefer; attending sporting events or watching them on television? Write a sentence to explain why.

Health and fitness

2.1 Read the advertisement for a fitness club. Underline words or phrases in the text that mean:

1 advantages	4 succeed in doing	7 trained
2 gets better	5 a course of exercises	8 advise
3 most modern	6 the right way to use something	9 very important

BODYLINE FITNESS CLUB

Regular exercise has lots of benefits. You become **stronger** and **healthier**, and you will even feel **more confident** about yourself as your general level of fitness improves.

Here at Bodyline we have a range of the latest exercise equipment to help you achieve this quickly and efficiently. This includes step machines, jogging machines, exercise bikes and weights.

When you join Bodyline, a personal trainer will design a fitness programme just for you. Your trainer will demonstrate the correct techniques so that you use the equipment safely and efficiently. There are always fully-qualified members of staff around to help if necessary.

We recommend at least 2–3 visits to the gym per week. It's important that you wear comfortable clothes when you exercise; a T-shirt and shorts or maybe a tracksuit are fine and trainers are essential. There are large lockers in the changing rooms. Afterwards you can relax in our sauna and steam room, or enjoy a healthy drink in the juice bar.

Your body needs to be active and fitness is fun so why not come along to Bodyline and find out more!

2.2 Look at the words in bold in the first paragraph of the text above and complete this table.

2.3 Now put the correct form of these adjectives into the sentences (1–6).

strong	*stronger*	strongest
healthy	*healthier*	
	more confident	*most ...*
		fittest

healthy   cheap   relaxing
lazy   fit   busy   expensive

1 I'm feeling ....*lazy*.......... today. Do you mind going to the gym without me?

2 Sunday is the .... day of the week at Bodyline because most people don't have to go to work. Let's go on Monday instead.

3 After I've been in the gym, I find sitting in the steam room .... than swimming up and down the pool.

4 Paul must be the .... member of staff at Bodyline. He's always using the machines.

5 A glass of fresh fruit juice is certainly .... than a cup of coffee.

6 Membership of a gym can be quite .... Football is much .... and more fun.

2.4 Make a list of gym equipment that is mentioned in the advertisement. Do you use a gym regularly? Do you think that it can be boring? Write a sentence explaining why or why not.

Exam practice

WRITING Part 1

Here are some sentences about going to a gym. For each sentence, complete the second sentence so that it means the same as the first. Use no more than three words.

Example

Jasmine had never been to the gym before.

It was <u>the first time</u> Jasmine had been to the gym.

Exam Tip

In this part your spelling must be correct. You will need to write up to three words.

1 Jasmine paid £45 for membership for three months.

Membership for 3 months .... Jasmine £45.

2 The trainer recommended using the gym two or three times a week.

'You .... the gym two or three times a week', said the trainer.

3 Jasmine was shown how to use the step machine by a member of staff.

A member of staff .... to use the step machine.

4 Jasmine enjoyed the exercise bike more than the jogging machine.

Jasmine found the exercise bike more .... the jogging machine.

5 Jasmine had a shower and then she went to the juice bar.

Jasmine went to the juice bar after she .... a shower.

LISTENING Part 3

13 **You will hear a radio announcement about a fun run. For each question, fill in the missing information in the numbered space.**

Exam Tip

If you don't hear the answer the first time, don't worry. Move on to the next question. In the exam the recording will be played twice so you will be able to check your answers and fill in any you missed the first time.

ABINGTON PARK FUN RUN

Time of the run: 11am

Date: Sunday, **(1)** ....

Venue: Abington Park

Distance: 3 kilometres

Race starts and finishes at the **(2)** .... in the park.

Facilities for changing in the **(3)** .... Club

Every runner gets a **(4)** ....

Cost of entry:

   Adults: £8 (in advance) / £10 (on the day)

   Children less than **(5)** .... years old:

                             no charge

Get an entry pack from any **(6)** ....

(or the website: <u>www.funrun.org</u>)

---

14 The natural world
Animals, the countryside

Animals

1.1 **Make a list of animals to put under these headings.**

insects   farm animals   wild animals   pets   sea creatures   birds

1.2 **Add these words to your lists in 1.1.**

bee   bull   goat   dolphin   zebra   cat   bear   dog
elephant   lion   pig   sheep   tiger   whale   parrot

1.3 **Write the name of the animal under the picture. Use a dictionary to help you if necessary.**

1 .... 2 .... 3 .... 4 .... 5 .... 6 .... 7 .... 8 ....

9 .... 10 .... 11 .... 12 .... 13 .... 14 .... 15 .... 16 ....

1.4 **Choose the best word for each gap (1–10). Which animal is being described?**

blood   teeth   fur   skin   sting   neck   tongue   wings   pets

1 This creature has two rows of very sharp ...._teeth_........ .

2 This animal has cold .... and smooth, dry ....

3 This pet has a very rough ....

4 This animal has orange and black .... and is the largest cat in the world.

5 This creature is not a bird but it has .... and flies well.

6 Some people keep these tiny, furry creatures as ....

7 This creature could give you a nasty ....

8 This animal has the longest .... in the world.

1.5 **Use the adjectives in the box to write sentences about the animals in 1.4 above.**

frightening   friendly   useful   beautiful   amusing   dangerous   interesting

I think the .... is a very .... animal because ....

1.6 Look at the questions below. Choose some of them to talk or write about in your notebook.

Pets: Are you an animal lover? Do you have a pet? What would be your ideal pet? Which animals make good pets and which ones do not? Why?

Wild animals: Which of the animals on page 62 have you seen and where? Which ones would you like to see and why?

The countryside

2.1 Read this text about New Zealand. Where did the text probably come from?

A   geography text book   B   a letter from a friend   C   a tourist information website

New Zealand

New Zealand is situated in the South Pacific Ocean and consists of two main islands – North Island and South Island. Both North and South Islands are full of hills and mountains. The north of the country and the east coast are rather more sunny than the far south. New Zealand's summer months are December to February, and this is an excellent time to visit the country's beautiful beaches, which are ideal for swimming, sunbathing, and diving. In autumn the forests and woods of Central Otago and Hawkes Bay are popular with visitors, with their colourful changing leaves and beautiful scenery.

There are also evergreen forests, which are home to the famous kiwi bird. This bird is flightless and therefore lives on the ground. It is a nocturnal creature, so if you want to see it digging in the ground with its long curved beak for insects, you will have to creep quietly into the forest at night. Winter is the best time to visit the mountains, either to ski or to enjoy the beautiful views of lakes and glaciers. In spring, new born lambs can be seen in the fields and the countryside is full of flowers. In fact, several cities celebrate the spring with a flower festival. If you like dangerous sports such as white water rafting, this is the time when melting snow makes river levels excitingly high.

2.2 Are these sentences true (*T*) or false (*F*), according to the text?

1   The weather is cloudier in the south. .....

2   Hawkes Bay is a good place for water sports. .....

3   The kiwi hides in the trees of the forests. .....

4   Spring is a good time to visit certain cities. .....

2.3 Now read the text in **2.1** again and find words which match the definitions below. Then write the word. You have been given the first letter to help you.

1   Young farm animals can be seen here in spring.
    f i e l d

2   In some countries, these freeze in winter and you can skate on them. l _ _ _ _

3   This is not as high as a mountain. h _ _ _

4   A piece of land which has the ocean all around it.
    i _ _ _ _ _

Vocabulary note

Guessing unknown words

If a text contains difficult and unknown words underline them then try to work out their meanings by looking at the context:

Look at **melting** in the last line of the text. You can see from the context that it is something that happens to snow in spring, and it makes the level of water in rivers rise. So you can guess that it means *turning from ice to water due to warmer temperatures*.

5   This is a good place to enjoy the sea. b _ _ _ _

6   A place where many trees grow together. f _ _ _ _ _

7   Some plants produce these in spring, others in summer. f _ _ _ _ _ _

8   Water flows in this from the mountains to the sea.
    r _ _ _ _

9   Land which is near the sea. c _ _ _ _

2.4 The same word fits in both gaps in each pair of sentences. Can you find the word for each pair?

1 A   A wood is similar to a .... but smaller.

  B   The Amazon is the world's largest rain ....

2 A   A stream is a small .... , often found in the mountains.

  B   A canal is a man-made .... used for transporting goods.

3 A   Farmers use hedges or fences to separate their ....

  B   Some .... have grass growing in them and others have corn or wheat.

2.5 Put these words into three groups according to their meanings.

star	soil	ocean	sun	sky	earth	universe	rock
planet	sand	lake	canal	stream	moon	river	sea

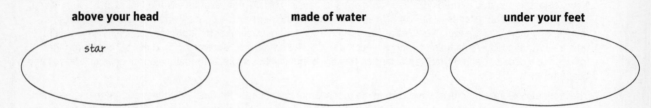

above your head   **made of water**   **under your feet**

star

2.6 Match the definition on the left with the correct word on the right.

1   A place to keep your boat.   CLIFF

2   You can walk or cycle along this.   VALLEY

3   You swim, sunbathe and have fun here.   HARBOUR

4   The space between two mountains.   CAVE

5   A high, steep wall of rock, often beside the sea.   PATH

6   A very dry place where few plants and animals live.   SEASIDE

7   A large hole under the ground or in a cliff or mountain.   DESERT

2.7 Each group of four words should remind you of another word. You have been given some of the letters of the word to help you. The first one has been done as an example.

leaf	branch	wood	forest	t r e e
collar	pet	bark	friend	_ o _
wings	fur	blind	cave	_ _ t
sand	beach	sun	holiday	s _ a _ _ _ e
flow	water	fish	Danube	_ i _ _ _
rose	plant	insect	garden	_ _ o _ e _
farm	lake	swim	eggs	_ u _ _
gate	grass	lambs	farmer	_ i _ _ _
high	rocks	climb	snow	_ _ _ n _ _ _ n
moon	stars	space	planets	_ _ i _ _ _ _ e
trees	wet	animals	Amazon	_ a _ _ _ _ r _ _ _
ships	waves	deep	dolphin	_ _ e _ _
ears	soft	fur	carrots	r _ b _ i _

Exam practice

LISTENING Part 1

1 🎧 **14a** **Which photograph are they looking at?**

A

B

C

2 **Where is Jim's house?**

A

B

C

3 **Which pets does Tony have?**

A

B

C

LISTENING Part 3

🎧 **14b** **You will hear a man giving some information about an animal park. For each question, fill in the missing information in the numbered space.**

Welldean Wild Animal Park

Opening times
10am – 6pm (April to September)
10am – **(1)** .... (October to March)

Animals
Many different kinds of animals to see, including a very rare
(2) ....

The Brown Bear
It comes from the forests of Europe and Asia.
It has a mainly vegetarian diet, but also eats
(3) .... , fish and small animals.

Safety
Do not open your car **(4)** .... while you are
travelling around the park.

Refreshments
The Café on the **(5)** .... serves fast food.

Supporting Welldean Wild Animal Park
To become a member of the Animal Club you must pay
(6) ....
Call 02785 453 7865 to find out about adopting an animal.

15 What's the weather like?

The weather, forecasting the weather, climates and seasons

The weather

sun   hot   storm   lightning
snow   sunshine   ice   fog   gale
heat   thunder   rain   cold

1.1 Look at the weather words. Check any you don't know in a dictionary. Which words can you use to describe each picture?

A    B    C

1.2 Match the two halves of the sentences.

1   Gales can   A   block roads.
2   Lightning can   B   cause floods.
3   Too much snow can   C   start fires.
4   A lot of rain can   D   blow down trees.

1.3 Change the nouns in the table below into adjectives by adding –y.

> ### Ⓥ *Vocabulary note*
>
> When turning nouns into adjectives, if the noun is spelt 'consonant, vowel, consonant', double the last letter and add –y:
>
> sun ⟶ sunny

noun	adjective
sun	
rain	
wind	
storm	
ice	
shower	
fog	
snow	
frost	
cloud	

1.4 Fill in the missing letters in the words in this sentence.

I looked at the _t_ _e r_ _ _ _m_ _ _ _ _ _ and saw that the _t_ _m_ _ _ _a u_ _ was 23 _d_ _ _ _r_ _ _s_ _c_ _ _t_ _g r_ _ _e.

1.5 Choose a noun or adjective from the exercises above to complete each sentence.

Example
*It was very cold and there was **snow** on the roofs.*

1   I had to be careful not to get burnt because the ....sun............ was very strong.

2   The .... was very frightening because I'm afraid of thunder and lightning.

3   It was easy to slip because the pavement was ....

4   The .... was more than 40 degrees.

5   There was so much .... that the streets began to look like rivers.

6   When I felt too .... , I went for a swim.

7   Every day of the holiday was bright and ....

8   When I looked at the .... I saw it was –10°C.

1.6 Match the sentences in **1.5** to the pictures in **1.1**.

Forecasting the weather

2.1 Match the words in the box with the definitions (A–E) and then use them to complete the sentences (1–5).

cool   mild   warm   wet   dry

A   Pleasant, not too hot: ....

B   Not as cold as expected: ....

C   No rain: ....

D   Pleasant, not too cold: ....

E   Lots of rain: ....

1   It will be hot again but there will be a .... wind blowing.

2   It's going to be .... again, so don't put away your umbrellas!

3   This month the weather has been surprisingly .... It's usually much colder than this.

4   The .... weather will continue into next week; perfect for a spring picnic.

5   It will be .... and sunny tomorrow. We don't expect rain until next week.

2.2 🎧 15a Listen to the weather forecast and number these words and phrases in the order you hear them. The first has been done for you as an example.

frost ......   fog ......
temperatures ......   cloudier ......
light winds ......   heavy rain ......
showers ..1..   snow ......
clear skies ......   bright sunshine ......

2.3 🎧 15a Listen again. What will the weather be like on each day? Draw lines between the days and the kind of weather.

Wednesday   Wednesday night   Thursday   Friday

wet   cold   sunny   dry   cloudy
frosty   snowy   foggy   windy

2.4 Which weather forecast (A–E) would be best for each person speaking?

I'm going to take part in a long distance running race on Saturday. The worst thing for me would be strong wind. I don't mind getting a bit wet. I would prefer that to sunshine.

I'm going sightseeing in Barcelona so I'm going to be walking around the city most of the day. I want the weather to be pleasant but not too hot.

I want to dig the garden and plant some seeds. If it doesn't rain, I will have to water the garden for a few days.

I've booked a four-day course to learn how to sail. If the weather isn't windy enough, or if it's too wet, they will cancel the course, which will be very disappointing.

I am going on a skiing holiday next week. Last year it was so sunny all the snow melted, so I really hope that doesn't happen again.

A   For the next few days the wind will be quite strong, but the weather will remain dry and not too cold. During the day there will be a mixture of cloud and sunshine.

B   Temperatures are dropping and snow is likely to fall in the mountains overnight. There will be plenty of sunshine and very little wind.

C   This weekend temperatures will be mild for the time of year. There will be a lot of cloud around, and possibly some light rain, but no wind.

D   The day will begin warm and sunny. During the afternoon clouds will arrive from the west and there will be some heavy showers in the early evening.

E   If you were planning on going to the beach you may be disappointed as temperatures are going to be cool for the time of year. However, it will be quite sunny and there is unlikely to be any wind.

2.5 What are your favourite activities? What are the best and worst weather conditions for those activities? Write or talk about your ideas.

2.6 Choose the best adjective.

1 Winds will probably be *light / weak* this weekend.

2 *Heavy / Strong* winds may cause problems for drivers of large vehicles.

3 Skies should remain *clean / clear* until Thursday.

4 Most areas will have *bright / high* sunshine for the next few days.

5 *Heavy / Strong* rain is expected in all parts of the country, so there is a danger of flooding.

6 There is likely to be some *light / weak* rain tomorrow, which is good news for gardeners.

7 We are expecting *tall / high* temperatures again this week, especially in the south.

8 Temperatures are very *low / light* for the time of year.

Climates and seasons

3.1 Write out these words in full. You have been given the first letter to help you.

A Points of the compass

N ____

N ____ W ____   N ____ E ____
W ____   E ____
S ____ W ____   S ____ E ____

S ____

> **Vocabulary note**
>
> Notice how these words are grouped together according to their meanings. Try storing words like this in your own vocabulary notebook as it will make it easier to learn and remember them.

B The seasons

w _____
s _____
s _____
a _____ or f ____
(US English)

C The months of the year

J _____   J ____
F _____   A ____
M ____   S _____
A ____   O _____
M __   N _____
J ____   D _____

> **Vocabulary note**
>
> The names of the months must always begin with a capital letter.

3.2 Match the countries in the box with the correct description (A–C).

Kenya   Ireland   Canada

A This country has mild winters and warm, but not hot, summers. The average temperature in summer is 15 degrees centigrade. Typical weather is clouds and rain. The warmest weather is in the south. ....

B Winter in this country is long and very cold, and summer is short and hot. On the coast, in places where the sea does not freeze, winter temperatures are warmer than inland. ....

C In this country the temperature does not vary much over the year, but some months are wetter than others. The central region has a lovely climate with long, warm sunny days. It is much hotter and drier in the north. ....

3.3 Now talk or write about the seasons and the weather in your country.

Exam practice

SPEAKING Part 2

It's winter and it's cold outside. Two of your friends want to do something together. Talk about the different things they could do together and decide which would be best. Here are some pictures to help you.

15b **Listen to two students doing this task and answer these questions.**

1 Did they mention every picture?

2 What reasons do they give for some of their decisions?

3 How do they ask for each other's opinion?

4 What do they agree would be the best thing to do?

WRITING Part 2

You want to invite your friend Sam to your country for a short visit. Write a postcard to send to Sam. In your postcard, you should:
• invite Sam to visit you.
• suggest a good time for Sam to come.
• say what the weather will be like when Sam comes.

Write 35–45 words.

Test Three (Units 11–15)

Choose the correct letter A, B or C.

1   Which of these subjects would you study in a laboratory?
    A chemistry   **B** drama   **C** geography

2   Which word means the **opposite** of *pointless*?
    A useful   **B** boring   **C** enjoyable

3   Where does a professor teach?
    A primary school   **B** secondary school   **C** university

4   Mr Wilson is a very .... teacher. He is always calm and never gets angry.
    A funny   **B** patient   **C** strict

5   I didn't feel ready to take the .... but I had no choice.
    A grade   **B** result   **C** exam

6   Everyone always pays .... in our history class.
    A attention   **B** progress   **C** interest

7   Jim had such a sore .... he could hardly speak.
    A headache   **B** cough   **C** throat

8   Mrs Jones phoned the doctor to arrange .... for that afternoon.
    A a dressing   **B** an appointment   **C** a prescription

9   Tim was fine but his car was .... in the accident.
    A damaged   **B** injured   **C** hurt

10 My clothes are all too loose now because I've .... so much weight.
    A put on   **B** lost   **C** taken off

11 A .... of fruit makes a more satisfying snack than a bar of chocolate.
    A piece   **B** can   **C** glass

12 You'll feel healthier if you ....
    A play more computer games   **B** eat more fried food   **C** take more exercise

13 Uncle Jack and Charlie .... fishing.
    A are doing   **B** have gone   **C** have done

14 Tina used to .... gymnastics at school.
    A practise   **B** play   **C** do

15 All the members of the hockey team must attend .... after school today.
   A practise   **B** exercise   **C** training

16 Which person does not play in a match?
   A coach   **B** captain   **C** partner

17 If you go to the gym .... your level of fitness will improve.
   A annually   **B** regularly   **C** normally

18 Early morning is the .... time at the swimming pool as most people prefer to stay in bed then.
   A quietest   **B** busiest   **C** fittest

19 Which of the following is NOT an insect?
   A bee   **B** fly   **C** bat

20 Which of the following is a farm animal?
   A camel   **B** monkey   **C** goat

21 Which of these has teeth, but no fur?
   A zebra   **B** snake   **C** parrot

22 The tiger is a very beautiful animal but it is very .... and people should not go near it.
   A dangerous   **B** amusing   **C** useful

23 This is a piece of land with water all around it.
   A island   **B** field   **C** hill

24 This is like a small, inland sea.
   A ocean   **B** lake   **C** river

25 Which of these types of weather has a lot of wind?
   A stormy   **B** icy   **C** foggy

26 Trees are often blown down by ....
   A thunder   **B** gales   **C** lightening

27 Average .... are rising in many parts of the world.
   A thermometers   **B** degrees   **C** temperatures

28 The rain was so .... over the weekend that the river flooded its banks.
   A strong   **B** heavy   **C** high

29 It looks like we are going to have a beautiful, ... day today.
   A clear   **B** clean   **C** light

30 The .... in countries like Colombia depends more on how high up you are, than the time of year.
   A season   **B** climate   **C** time

16 The media

Television, reading books, newspapers and magazines

Television

1.1 Match the programme types (1–8) to the descriptions (A–H).

Type of television programme

1 wildlife documentary
2 historical documentary
3 current affairs programme
4 quiz show
5 cartoon
6 'sitcom' (situation comedy)
7 soap (soap opera)
8 thriller

Description

A *a series, on several times a week, that follows the lives of a group of people*

B *a weekly programme showing a group of characters in different amusing situations*

C *competitors answer questions to win a prize*

D *exciting drama usually involving a murder*

E *film that shows events that really happened in the past*

F *programme about important events that are happening at the present time*

G *film about animals and plants*

H *film, often for children, that uses drawings instead of real people*

1.2 Look at the list of TV programmes for this evening. What sort of programme is each one (1–8)?

CHANNEL 1	CHANNEL 2
6pm Home Farm: Will Eddie be able to stop Lisa from telling James the truth? **1) ....**	**5:30 Bertie Bear:** Further adventures of the lovable little pink bear. **5) ....**
7:30 My Family: More laughs as Nick gets a job painting litter bins and Susan invites her mother to stay. **2) ....**	**6pm** News and Weather
8pm Our planet: Insect eaters, penguins and butterflies **3) ....**	**7pm Roundup:** General knowledge questions with quizmaster, Les Bunyan. **6) ....**
9pm Discovery: Paul Fox introduces the French scientists who discovered the real shape of the earth in 1735. **4) ....**	**9pm Conviction:** Detective Harrison finds the killer and brings him before the judge. **7) ....**
10pm National news and weather, followed by local news.	**10pm The week:** Politicians discuss this week's developments in parliament. **8) ....**

1.3 Complete the text by choosing the best answer from page 73 for each space (1–10).

My Family

'My Family' is a popular weekly television comedy
(1) ....*series*........ based on a supposedly
(2) .... British family. Life is certainly
never **(3)** .... in their house. The father,
Ben, is a dentist who spends most of his time
(4) .... about his kids, while Susan, his
wife, is **(5)** .... at cooking and wants
to control everyone's lives. Lazy Nick, the oldest
son, tries out increasingly **(6)** .... jobs,
daughter Janey is crazy about fashion and is always
(7) .... her parents for money. Michael is
the clever teenager, looking for a girlfriend and
(8) .... to keep out of his father's way.
This show has strong **(9)** .... placed
in embarrassing and amusing, but still believable,
situations – the perfect ingredients for a long-
running **(10)** ....

1	series / channel / set	6	unsuitable / unnecessary / untidy
2	actual / current / typical	7	demanding / asking / questioning
3	usual / dull / common	8	patient / jealous / anxious
4	annoying / complaining / disappointing	9	characters / heroes / roles
5	horrible / difficult / terrible	10	soap / sitcom / drama

1.4 How often do you watch television? What sort of programmes do you like? What are the most popular soaps and sitcoms in your country?

Reading books

2.1 Do you enjoy reading? Where and when do you like to read? Look at the people in these pictures. Complete these sentences:

I think the best time for reading is ....
....
In my opinion, the best place for reading
is ....
....

2.2 Here are some types of books. Circle the ones that are non-fiction.

romantic novels   science fiction   biography   adventure stories
cookbooks   historical novels   horror stories   fantasy novels
travel books   thrillers   mysteries

What types of books do you enjoy reading? Underline them in the box above.

2.3 🔊 16 Listen to Ruby and Federico talking about the books they like to read. Underline any words from **2.2** that you hear.

2.4 🔊 16 Listen again and complete columns 1 and 2 in the table below.

	1 Ruby	2 Federico	3 You
My usual time and place for reading			
Number of hours I spend reading per week			
Books I like			
Books I don't like			
The last book I read			

2.5 Complete Ruby and Federico's questions.

Ruby: Would you mind .... ?

My first question is .... ? I read early in the morning.

How .... ? How many .... spend reading?

This is the interesting bit – what .... ?

Federico: I think you can learn a lot from non-fiction .... ?

Ruby: Fiction's perfect for relaxing, don't .... ?

Here's my final question. What .... ?

Federico: It was science fiction. Would you .... ?

2.6 Go back to **2.4** and complete column 3 of the table using the words that you have practised in this unit.

> **Error warning!**
>
> **lend** and **borrow**
> Don't confuse these two verbs. When you **lend** something to somebody they **borrow** it from you: *When Federico lends the book to Ruby, Ruby is borrowing the book from him.*

Newspapers and magazines

3.1 How often? Complete the second statement so that it means the same as the first.

1 *The Times* newspaper comes out every day.

The Times is a ....daily......... newspaper.

2 It has a colour magazine once a week.

It has a .... colour magazine.

3 There is also a fortnightly sports magazine.

The sports magazine appears every .... weeks.

4 *Marie Claire* is published each month.

Marie Claire is a .... magazine.

5 The company calendar is produced annually.

The company produces a calendar .... a year.

3.2 Can you find these words in the wordsnake below?

1 His job is to write about the news. ....

2 A piece of writing in a newspaper or magazine. ....

3 This drawing makes fun of the news. ....

4 A piece of writing about a film, book or theatre event. ....

5 A picture taken with a camera. ....

6 You'll find the football results here. ....

7 The words in big letters at the top of the page ....

treviewtheadlineshinjournalisticarticlescartoonisphotographstisportsreportide

3.3 What do these headlines mean? Choose the best explanation.

1 **2,600 travel jobs lost as passengers book flights on the internet**

A A travel firm has lost applications from 2,600 people for jobs as computer operators.

B 2,600 passengers who booked air travel on the internet lost their seats on the flights.

C Because people are arranging their flights online, 2,600 travel agents have become unemployed.

2 **Troublemakers in city centre to get immediate £80 police fines during the holiday period**

A Anyone who behaves badly in public during the holiday will have to pay £80 straight away.

B During the holidays the police will charge £80 to deal with any problems in the city centre.

C The police will prevent trouble by charging people £80 to enter the city centre.

3 **Footballer calls for help to find stolen dogs**

A A footballer has found some dogs that were stolen and wants people to help him find the owners.

B A footballer, whose dogs have disappeared, wants the public to help him get them back.

C A footballer, who the police think has stolen some dogs, wants help in finding the real thief.

Exam practice

READING Part 4

- Read the text and questions below.
- For each question, mark the correct letter, A, B, C or D.

Sports Journalist

A few years ago my newspaper sent me to China to report on the World Student Games in Beijing. Everywhere I went I was questioned by journalism students: how much money did I earn? How many countries had I visited? Had I met David Beckham? In China sports reporting is seen as a dream job and Chinese students are fascinated by foreign sports reporters.

Several years later I visited China again to write about a major motor race in Shanghai. At the track I saw one of those former students, Jie Xeng. He was working for one of China's largest news agencies so I asked him about his life as a sports writer.

'Sometimes it is wonderful', he replied, 'but there is a lot of travel, a lot of stress and sometimes sports people are not very helpful.'

Jie had discovered one of the hard truths about life as a sports writer. You might think all you need are writing skills and a knowledge of sport. These are certainly essential, but you also need to be prepared for any number of problems.

On that visit to Shanghai for example, the journey from my hotel to the race-track took at least three hours, through heavy traffic. For four days, I followed racing drivers and organisers around but they were too busy to give me more than a one-word answer. Then I would write my report and send it to London. When I finally got back to my hotel at night, everything, including the restaurant, was closed.

Being a sports writer may appear to be a fantastic job but there are as many difficult situations as there are magic moments!

---

1 What is the writer's main purpose in this article?
   A to inform readers about visiting China
   B to encourage young people to travel
   C to give a realistic description of his work
   D to warn students about newspaper careers

2 Why did the writer travel to China the first time?
   A He was sent there by his employers.
   B He hoped to interview some famous sportsmen.
   C He was invited to give a lecture about journalism.
   D He was going to take part in an athletics competition.

3 When he met the writer the second time, Jie Xeng …
   A was working for a motor-racing organisation.
   B no longer wanted to be a journalist.
   C didn't recognise the writer at first.
   D had completed his university studies.

4 What does the writer say about the Shanghai motor race?
   A The race track was easy to get to.
   B There was a good hotel nearby.
   C No-one had time to talk to him.
   D He had problems contacting London.

5 What might the writer say to his friends?
   A 'There aren't many people who get paid for doing their hobby. Aren't you jealous?'
   B 'Sports people are always keen to give interviews, which makes my job even more enjoyable.'
   C 'I don't know why you complain about travelling to work every day. It's easy compared to the places I visit.'
   D 'Poor Jie Xeng. He used to be so anxious to be a journalist and now all he wants is to give it up.'

17 Around town

Towns and cities, places and buildings, vehicles

Towns and cities

1.1 Do you live in the city or the countryside? Make sentences to talk about where you live.

| I like it | (where I live) | because | it is (very) … |
| I don't like it | (in my village / town / city) | | of the … |

quiet   traffic jams   dirty   noise   crowded   pollution   busy   safe   convenient
exciting   beautiful   public transport   clean   scenery   lively   peace and quiet
atmosphere   dangerous   boring

1.2 Look at the diagram and label it with the words below.

turning
crossroads
roundabout
pedestrian crossing
signpost
traffic lights
bus stop
corner

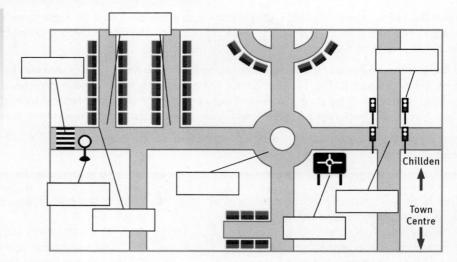

1.3 Read this information from Jack telling his friend how to get to his house. Mark Jack's house with a cross on the diagram.

You can cycle to my house from the town centre quite easily, but be careful because the road is very busy. When you leave the town centre, follow the signs for Chillden. After about 10 or 15 minutes you'll come to a big crossroads with traffic lights. Turn left there. You'll see a signpost on your left and then you will come to a roundabout. Go straight over the roundabout. You'll see two turnings on the right. The second one is mine, just opposite the bus stop. There's a big tree on the corner, you can't miss it. Anyway, if you go over the pedestrian crossing then you know you've gone too far. My house is the third on the left.

1.4 Pick another house on the diagram and write an email giving directions on how to get there from the town centre.

Places and buildings

2.1 Match the places on the left with the reason people visit them on the right.

Places	Reasons to visit
factory, office	to do some shopping
mosque, church, cathedral	to visit a doctor
university, school, college	to dance and have fun in the evening
stadium, theatre, cinema	to learn and study
castle, ruin, palace	to have something to eat or drink
museum, gallery	to take some exercise
sports centre, swimming pool	to spend the night
clinic, hospital	to go to work
café, coffee shop, restaurant	to say a prayer
guesthouse, hotel	to watch a performance
nightclub, disco, bar	to do some sightseeing
supermarket, department store, bookshop	to look at beautiful objects and paintings

> **Error warning!**
>
> **library, bookshop**
> You borrow books from a **library** or go there to read or study. If you want to buy a book you go to a **bookshop**.

2.2 Put the words in the box below into the gaps in 1–5 and then match each sentence to the right place.

fuel	wallet	criminals	~~swings~~	letters	judge	stamps	court	parcels

1 Children love to play on the ....swings........ here.

2 If your .... was stolen while you were shopping, you would go here.

3 This is where .... are sent by the .... after they have been to ....

4 You can buy .... , and post .... and .... here.

5 You can get .... for your car here.

PETROL STATION

PRISON

PLAYGROUND

POLICE STATION

POST OFFICE

2.3 Find words in the wordsnake, circle them and then match them to the clues below.

saving money   ~~repairing cars~~   buying magazines   getting medicine
seeing animals   selling fruit and vegetables   lying on the grass   reading books

sdkjhfykioskaiurthnwlibraryheuipskzoojwyebgarageryehcgfwopharmacyieufagumarketksjdfuehvbankoufijparkkxjcvu

2.4 Unscramble the letters to make words that match the definitions. The first and last letters are in the right place.

1 This looks and sounds lovely in a town square. FNTIUAON ....

2 You travel through this to go through mountains or under rivers. TNEUNL ....

3 This goes over rivers or valleys. BGIDRE ....

4 You can climb up this to get a good view of the city. TWEOR ....

5 This is beside the road and is for pedestrians to walk on. PMVEEANT ....

6 This is often made of stone or metal and can be in the shape of a person. SUTATE ....

7 You walk through this under a busy road. (in the US it is for underground trains.) SBWUAY ....

2.5 Why would you go to these people? Make some sentences.

> dentist   hairdresser   dry cleaner   newsagent   chemist

Example:
I would go to the newsagent if I needed to buy a newspaper.

2.6 🔊 17 Listen to a girl talking about her town. Which of the following is NOT mentioned?

> shopping   going out   art and culture   getting around the town   doing sport

2.7 🔊 17 Now listen again and decide if these sentences are true (*T*) or false (*F*).

1   The centre of town is not very attractive. ..F..

2   The public transport is good. .....

3   There are lots of places to eat, drink and dance. .....

4   The theatre, cinema and art gallery are all in one building. .....

5   The museum is rather boring. .....

6   Sports facilities in the town are quite limited. .....

7   There are plenty of places to play football. .....

Vehicles

3.1 Look at the list of vehicles in the box and answer the questions (1–6) below.

> bus   train   car   taxi   tram   bicycle (bike)   ship   cab   aeroplane (plane)   motorbike   helicopter   hovercraft   coach   lorry   scooter   ferry   truck   underground train

1   Find two that fly.

2   Find two vehicles that travel on rails.

3   Find three that you can catch and miss.

4   Find two pairs of words that have very similar meanings.

5   Find three different kinds of boat. What is the difference between them?

6   What is the difference between a bus and a coach, and between a motorcycle and a scooter?

3.2 Now answer these questions about the vehicles in **3.1**.

a   Which of these vehicles do you or members of your family own?

b   Which ones can you pay to use in your town, city or village?

c   Which one(s) have you not travelled in yet?

d   Which ones do you enjoy / hate travelling in / on?

3.3 Each group of four words should remind you of another word. Which word? You have been given some of the letters to help you.

1   cabin   sail   deck   seats   _ o _ _

2   wings   toilet   cabin   windows   _ _ a _ _

3   wheels   handlebars engine   number plate   c _ _ _ _ _ _

4   tyres   handlebars bell   chain   _ _ c _ _ _

5   engine   seats   toilet   air conditioning   _ o _ _ _

6   brake   boot   seatbelt   windscreen   _ _ _ r

Exam practice

READING Part 1

Look at the text in each question. What does it say? Choose the correct letter, A, B or C.

1

> QUEUE HERE FOR MUSEUM TOUR.
> TICKETS MUST BE PURCHASED IN
> ADVANCE FROM RECEPTION.

If you wish to join the tour of the museum you should …
A   buy a ticket from the guide.
B   get a ticket before joining the queue.
C   join the queue at reception.

2

> Do not climb on this
> statue as it is easy to
> damage the stone.

The purpose of this notice is to …
A   inform people of the danger of climbing on the statue.
B   request that people keep off the statue to avoid harming it.
C   describe damage that has been caused by people climbing on the statue.

3

> Please remember to take
> all your belongings with
> you when you leave the
> changing-room.

Visitors are asked to make sure …
A   they leave nothing behind after using the changing-room.
B   the changing-room is clean and tidy when they leave.
C   their belongings are safe while they are in the changing-room.

SPEAKING Part 3

Look at the photograph below. When you are ready, practise speaking for one minute about the picture.

> ### Exam Tip
>
> Ask yourself these questions to help you think of things to say.
> *What can you see in the picture?*
> (vehicles, buildings etc.)
> *Do you live in a place like this?*
> *If not, would you like to live in a place like this?*

18 What's on?
The arts, theatre and music, cinema

The arts

1.1 ⊕ 18 Look at the words about entertainment and the arts in the box. Listen to a man talking on the radio and underline the words that you hear.

ballet   classical   concert   comedy   dance   drama   novel   film   jazz   orchestra   musical   exhibition   opera   play   poem

1.2 ⊕ 18 Listen again and complete the notes below.

This week at Highgate Arts Centre

Monday: *Birds on the wing* – Play from the **(1)** ....novel......... by Philip Cruise.

Tuesday: Salsa workshop with Diana Fransen. Join in a mix of dance and **(2)** .... to Latin American **(3)** ....

Wednesday: Matsuri drummers from Japan. Amazing **(4)** .... and **(5)** .... effects.

Thursday: Highgate Silver Band, under their leader Leslie Ager, present a concert of popular **(6)** .... music with requests from the **(7)** ....

Friday: Maddie Felix: The **(8)** .... singer and guitarist is on a concert tour to celebrate her new CD.

Saturday: *Beauty and the Beast:* A **(9)** .... for all ages.

All week: Sea **(10)** .... by local artists in the coffee shop gallery.

1.3 Answer the questions (1–5) below:

1   On which days can you hear music?

2   Which shows can the audience take part in?

3   On which day can you see a theatre performance?

4   When is the art exhibition?

5   Which show would you choose to go to. Why?

1.4 Put the right form of *see / look (at) / watch* or *listen (to) / hear* into the sentences.

1   I .... the latest James Bond film at the cinema last night.

2   My friend wants to wait until it comes out on DVD and then .... it at home.

3   It is said that people only spend about 3 seconds .... each picture in an exhibition.

4   We couldn't afford tickets for the concert so we stood outside. We .... everything perfectly but we couldn't .... anything.

 Vocabulary note

listen (to), hear
You can hear something without listening to it.
I was listening to a CD and didn't hear the phone ring.
I'm sorry – I wasn't listening. I didn't hear what you said.
see / look (at) / watch
You **look** when you are trying to **see** something.
You **watch** something that moves.
If you see a film or play, you go to the cinema / theatre to **watch** or **see** it.
Have you seen the new James Bond film yet?
Sally looked everywhere but she didn't see her colleague at the football match because he was watching it on TV at home.

5   I've .... Maddie Felix on the radio but I've never .... her live on stage.

6   I .... the magician closely to try to discover how he performed the trick.

Theatre and music

2.1 Complete these notices, which you might see in a theatre, using words and phrases from the box on the right.

A

Tickets booked .... or by phone must be collected from the .... at least half an hour before the performance starts.

admitted	audience	box office
equipment	interval	mobile phones
online	performance	record	theatre

B

Latecomers will not be .... to the performance until the ....

C

Members of the .... are requested to turn off .... and not to unwrap sweets during the ....

Vocabulary note

un–

We can add the letters **un–** to the front of words to make them mean the opposite:
I'll **unwrap** that sweet for you.
The cowboy **untied** his horse, jumped on its back and rode away.
Don't use this ladder; it's **unsafe**.

D

Anyone attempting to .... this performance will be requested to leave the .... and their .... will be removed.

2.2 These people appear in the theatre or concert hall. Make words ending in –er, –or, –ian or –ist.

Example:

A s _ _ _ _ _ _ uses his or her voice to perform different types of music. _s i n g e r_

1 A g _ _ _ _ _ _ _ _ _ plays classical, rock, pop or jazz on an instrument with six strings.

2 A c _ _ _ _ _ _ _ _ tells jokes to make the audience laugh.

3 The d _ _ _ _ _ _ _ sits at the back of the band and often plays quite loudly.

4 Anyone who sings or plays an instrument is a m _ _ _ _ _ _ _ _ .

5 The d _ _ _ _ _ _ _ _ is in charge of putting on a play or a film.

6 A p _ _ _ _ _ _ _ makes music on a keyboard.

7 An a _ _ _ _ plays a character on the stage or in a film.

2.3 Complete this letter with the words in the box.

audience	star	act	clapped	comedy
costumes	curtain	lighting	make-up
role	sound	scene	scenery

Dear Suzie,

I've just been to the theatre. I saw a (1) .... about a crazy family living in an old castle. The (2) .... of the 90-year-old grandfather was actually played by a man in his 20s. His (3) .... was very good – they managed to make him look really old. The (4) .... of the show was the little girl who played the youngest daughter. The (5) .... loved her. The best (6) .... was when the old man thought there were burglars in the middle of the night. The theatre group had made their own (7) .... and (8) .... There were some great (9) .... and (10) .... effects.

At the end everyone (11) .... for ages, even after the (12) .... had come down.

I'd like to be an actor – have you ever been in a play?

Love, Mia

Cinema

3.1 Here are some words that we use to describe types of films.

> action   animation   cartoon   comedy   drama
> fantasy   historical   horror   mystery   romantic
> science fiction   thriller

Look at the pictures and decide what type of films they are from. You can use more than one word from the box. What is your favourite film? What type of film is it?

> ### Exam Tip
>
> If you meet a word that you don't know, for example *horror* or *fantasy*, think of similar words (*horrible* and *fantastic* for example). They will often help you work out the meaning.

3.2 Read this film review. Find words that mean:

1 a group of films with the same characters

2 the main character

3 a short part of a film

4 a person who hates you

5 amazing pictures and sounds made by using special techniques

---

Harry Potter and the Goblet of Fire

This is the fourth film in the Harry Potter series. The hero, Harry, is a young magician at Hogwarts school, who has to fight against his old enemy, Lord Voldemort.

In this film Harry meets some of his most difficult challenges so far. There are plenty of hair-raising adventures and excellent special effects, which audiences will enjoy, although some may be a little too frightening for younger children.

In this film Harry and his friends, Ron and Hermione, are growing up and as well as the familiar scenes of fun at school, there is some teenage romance when Harry and Ron have to find partners for the Hogwarts dance.

Fans of the book may feel a little disappointed as some details are left out. But in general the director has done a great job and this is a fast-moving, action-packed film.

3.3 Which words can you think of to complete these sentences?

1 The director .... a film.

2 A film star .... in a film.

3 The film is .... at the cinema.

3.4 Look again at the last line of the review: *a fast-moving, action-packed film*. A *fast-moving film* is a film where the events move fast. An *action-packed film* is a film packed with action. What is / are ...

1 hair-raising adventures?   2 a breath-taking scene?   3 a nail-biting thriller?

3.5 How could you describe ...

1 a story that never ends?

2 a woman who is dressed well?

3 a film that runs for a long time?

4 a child who behaves well?

5 a film star who is famous all over the world?

Exam practice

READING Part 3

Look at the sentences below about making films. Read the text underneath. If the sentence is correct put A, if it is incorrect put B.

1 Film-makers prefer to use university buildings during term time. ☐
2 A University of London building has appeared in an American film series. ☐
3 Film makers often completely change the appearance of the buildings they use. ☐
4 Filming *A Clockwork Orange* at Brunel University only required a small production team. ☐
5 Kubrick was satisfied with the scenes he filmed during the three weeks at Brunel University. ☐
6 The universities of Oxford and Cambridge refuse to allow filming to take place in their buildings. ☐
7 The University of Southern California can be seen in a number of well-known films. ☐
8 It is less expensive to make films in Canada than in the United States. ☐
9 Universities welcome the opportunity to get some income from their buildings. ☐
10 Students are sometimes offered parts in films being made at their universities. ☐

Making films at university

An increasing number of universities on both sides of the Atlantic are becoming film locations. Many universities have fantastic buildings and there are long holidays when they are empty. This allows film-makers a period of uninterrupted time to shoot a film.

In most cases the universities do not appear as themselves. Londoners were surprised to see American police cars cruising around in front of the University Library, which was used as the Gotham City police offices in all the Batman movies. London University Library is a classic example of 1930s architecture and has become a popular location for a large number of films and television series set in that period.

Usually the buildings are dressed up so that they cannot be recognised easily. Thirty years ago a lecture theatre at Brunel university was used in Stanley Kubrick's frightening film about the future, *A Clockwork Orange*. At that time its huge grey blocks were considered very modern. Kubrick thought that it would be perfect for the headquarters of the secret police. For three weeks there were at least 200 people on the site – electricians, carpenters, make-up people, set builders. Everything went well until some time later, Kubrick decided he was unhappy with his work and wanted to re-shoot some scenes. They had to go back, rebuild the set and do the scenes again. It caused a lot of trouble as term had already started.

Oxford and Cambridge are the most popular universities with both students and film-makers and both find it equally difficult to get into them. Some excellent films have been made there, most recently the Harry Potter films.

Across the Atlantic, a number of actors and directors are former students of the University of Southern California. Perhaps that is why its buildings have been used in more major films than any other educational institution in the USA. Recently however, American film crews have moved to Canada because of lower production costs there. The University of Toronto has played the role of two more famous US universities – Massachusetts Institute of Technology in *Good Will Hunting* and Harvard in *Skulls*.

Universities encourage this alternative use of their buildings and see it as a useful way of earning some extra money. From the director's point of view, universities make fantastic locations for feature films, television dramas, advertisements and still photography, such as fashion pictures.

Unfortunately, being a student at one of these universities is unlikely to be helpful for a future career in acting. Most film shoots take place in the holidays and film-makers always bring their own professional actors to play students!

19 Technology
Communicating, computers

Communicating

email   face to face   landline
hand-written letter   text   mobile

1.1 Match the words in the box to the pictures (A–F).

A    B 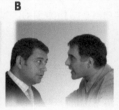   C    D    E    F

1.2 Now complete these sentences with the words from 1.1.

1   Older relatives usually appreciate a .... thanking them for a present.

2   If I'm going to be late for an appointment I call on my .... to say when I'll arrive.

3   I use the .... in the evening if I want a nice long chat with one of my friends.

4   I'm going to .... my teacher and explain why I can't finish my essay on time.

5   The best way to give someone instructions is to speak to them ....

6   If somebody sends me a good joke I .... it to all my friends.

1.3 What's your opinion? Make your own sentences using words from each column.

| A call on the landline
An email
A text message
A hand-written letter
A mobile phone call
A face to face
  conversation | is the | quickest
cheapest
kindest
easiest
worst
most personal
most reliable
most difficult | way | to send the same information to a large number of people.
to congratulate someone on passing their exams.
to speak to someone in another country.
to let the boss know you've been held up in traffic.
to tell your boyfriend you don't love him any more.
to let your parents know you've arrived safely at your
  destination. |

Computers

2.1 How much time do you spend on the computer each day? Do you use a computer for any of the activities in the box? Add to this list any other activities you use a computer for.

homework   surfing the internet   computer games   sending emails
internet chatrooms   downloading music   online shopping

2.2 Look at these verbs that are used with computers. Put the correct form of the verb in the sentences. Check any you don't know in a dictionary.

access	download	~~crash~~	delete
print	save	surf	

1 I'm sorry I haven't done my homework. There was a thunderstorm and my computer ......*crashed*...... .

2 Always remember to .... any changes you've made to your work before you shut down your computer.

3 Some people .... their emails as soon as they've read them but I prefer to keep them for about a month.

4 Sam took lots of pictures at the party but he hasn't .... them from his camera onto his computer yet.

5 You can discover an amazing amount of information by .... the internet.

6 You have to register with a password before you can .... some sites.

7 I always check my essay carefully for mistakes before I finally .... it off and hand it in.

2.3 **🔊 19a** Listen to two people, Eva and Carl, talking about computers. Underline the activities in **2.1** that they mention.

2.4 Read sentences 1–5 below and make compound nouns.

Example:
My big, old computer has finally broken and I'm going to replace it with a ....*laptop*.......... . (a computer that's small enough to use on top of your lap)

1 This table's very shiny so the mouse won't work properly. Have we got a ....? (a *mat* to put the *mouse* on)

2 Some people .... music from the internet and play it on an MP3 player. (transfer or *load down* from one computer system to another)

3 I've forgotten my .... so I can't open my email. (a secret *word* that lets you enter or *pass* into a computer)

4 You have to be careful if you use a .... because you don't know who you may be talking to. (place on the internet for *chatting* with other users)

5 If I don't use my computer for 60 seconds the .... appears. (a moving pattern to prevent, or *save* the *screen* from damage)

2.5 Read this text and choose the correct words to complete it.

Smart homes

Mitsuko Ohno and her 10-month-old daughter Kayoko **(1)** *recently / lately* moved into their new house in Nagoya in Japan. From the **(2)** *outside / outdoors* it looks just like any other house, but this house was built using the very latest technology. Mitsuko controls all the **(3)** *equipment / equipments* in her flat with a mini-computer, which she wears on her wrist like a watch. This mini computer also measures Mitsuko's electricity, **(4)** *pays / pays for* her bills, and stores video messages. It gives her **(5)** *informations / information* about when the washing machine has finished or who is at the door.

Mitsuko's fridge has a **(6)** *screen / scene* that provides **(7)** *receipts / recipes* for the ingredients inside, and lets her know if the food is **(8)** *out of date / out of order*. The bedroom mirror displays her timetable for the day, helps her choose her **(9)** *cloths / clothes* and brings her the latest weather and traffic news. When it's time to go to work, everything in this home of the future automatically turns itself off.

Which of the meanings in the Vocabulary note opposite does 'smart' have in the text heading above?

> **Ⓥ** *Vocabulary note*
>
> **smart** can mean …
> 1 *containing a mini-computer or microchip*
> 2 *fashionable and well-dressed*
> 3 *clever*

2.6 Look at these three sentences. Which meaning of *smart* (1, 2 or 3 from the Vocabulary note on page 85) matches which sentence (A, B or C)?

A   Sam's a very **smart** boy. He always gets top marks in tests. .....

B   Eva always looks **smart**, even if she's just taking her dog for a walk. .....

C   The hotel gave us a **smart** card which we used as a room key and to pay for food and drinks in the restaurant. .....

2.7   ⏺ 19b Listen to this advertisement for a computer. Circle the numbers that you hear.

16	2.36	23.6	263	2.57	2.75
275	2.63	30.25	32.5	60	
500.12	512	5,012	£637.45	£645.37	
£749.50	£7,490.50	54.00	5,400		

> **Ⓥ** *Vocabulary note*
>
> Remember that thousands are separated from hundreds by a comma.
> *Two thousand four hundred and fifty three* is written *2,453*.
> A decimal point is shown by a full stop. *One point five* is written *1.5*.

2.8   ⏺ 19b Listen again and complete these notes.

LAPBOOK

Measurements:
Width of screen   1 .... cm
Thickness   2 .... cm
Weight   3 .... kg
Memory   4 .... megabytes
Hard drive   5 .... gigabytes
Speed   6 .... rpm
Price   7 £.........................
                      8 £......................... (including tax)

2.9   Now write the numbers as words.

1 ....
2 ....
3 ....
4 ....
5 ....
6 ....
7 ....
8 ....

2.10   📖 These common words have very different meanings when they are used with computers.

application   cut   keyboard   memory   paste   programme   RAM   web   window   virus

Check any words you don't know in a dictionary and complete this poem. One word is used twice.

Do you remember when a computer
Was something from a science fiction show?
A .... was something you hated to clean
And .... was the cousin of a goat.
An .... was for employment,
And a .... a TV show.
You lost your .... with age
And a .... was part of a piano.
.... was what you did with a knife,
And .... would make things stick,
A .... was a spider's home.
And a .... meant you were sick.

Maybe I'll stay with my notebook
And the .... in my head
In case my computer crashes – I don't want to end up dead!

Exam practice

LISTENING Part 4

19a **Look at the six sentences for this part. You will hear a girl, Eva, and a boy, Carl, talking about computers. Decide if each sentence is correct or incorrect. If it is correct, put _A_. If it is not correct, put _B_.**

1 Carl uses his computer for a maximum of two hours each evening.

2 Eva is worried that surfing the internet is taking up too much of her time.

3 Carl warns Eva that some information on the internet is unreliable.

4 Eva and Carl both agree that chatrooms are a good way to make new friends.

5 Carl's friend sometimes comes to his house to play computer games late at night.

6 Carl and Eva both decide to limit the amount of time they spend online.

> **Exam Tip**
>
> If you don't know the answer to a question go on to the next one. You can check any answers you have missed the second time you hear the recording.

WRITING Part 1

Here are some sentences about computer games. For each question, complete the second question so that it means the same as the first. Use no more than three words.

Example

A lot of Jack's computer games are downloaded from the internet.
Jack _downloads_ a lot of computer games from the internet.

1 Jack and his friend Ed both like car-theft computer games.
Jack likes car-theft computer games and .... his friend Ed.

2 Ed wanted to know if Jack had got all the Mario computer games.
'Jack, ... got all the Mario computer games?' asked Ed.

3 Jack and Ed found the special effects in _Rainbow 6_ amazing.
Jack and Ed were .... the special effects in _Rainbow 6_.

4 Jack stopped playing _Jungle Party_ because he found it so childish.
Jungle Party was .... a childish game that Jack stopped playing it.

5 Adventure games are not usually as noisy as war games.
War games are usually .... adventure games.

6 Jack's little sister is too young to play computer games.
Jack's little sister isn't .... to play computer games.

> **Exam Tip**
>
> This part tests grammar and spelling. Check that your answer has the same meaning as the first sentence and that you have used the correct verb tense.

20 Working life

Jobs, applying for a job, business and industry

Jobs

1.1 Divide the jobs in the box into three groups with the following headings:

- **Professions** (You need a university degree):
- **Trades** (You must be specially trained):
- **Unskilled jobs** (No special training or skills needed):

architect   carpenter   engineer   labourer
lawyer   mechanic   security guard
dentist   porter   hairdresser   chef
journalist   butcher   pharmacist   cleaner

1.2 Look at the jobs above and answer these questions. Who ...?

1 keeps buildings safe at night
2 cooks food in a restaurant
3 carries suitcases in hotels
4 repairs people's cars
5 writes stories for newspapers
6 makes things out of wood

1.3 Which of the people below are performers?

actor   comedian   artist   novelist   designer
dancer   singer   TV presenter   musician
cameraman   film star   disc jockey   poet

1.4 Write the names of one or more jobs from **1.3** beside each of the following. Who has to ...?

1 be good at telling jokes
2 be an excellent writer
3 have a beautiful voice
4 look good all the time
5 be able to draw
6 be able to play an instrument

1.5 Make at least eight correct sentences.

A	publisher detective newsagent farmer nurse policeman librarian judge doctor chemist waiter teacher	deals with works in looks after serves	the public. the countryside. criminals. books. a shop. ill people. children

1.6 Match a noun in the first column (1–8) to a noun in the second column (A–F) to make eight jobs.

1	flight		
2	fire	A	assistant
3	travel	B	attendant
4	sales	C	agent
5	shop	D	operator
6	customs	E	fighter
7	police	F	officer
8	machine		

1.7 Can you work out what these jobs are?

1 A m _ _ _ _ _ wears and shows off the latest fashions.
2 A p _ _ _ _ _ flies planes.
3 A s _ _ _ _ _ _ _ works in the army.
4 A s _ _ _ _ _ works on a ship.
5 A p _ _ _ _ _ _ delivers letters and parcels.
6 A d _ _ _ _ _ helps ill people get better.
7 A t _ _ _ _ _ _ gives lessons in school.
8 An i _ _ _ _ _ _ _ _ _ _ translates as you speak.
9 A c _ _ _ _ _ _ is in charge of a ship.

1.8 **Choose the best word to complete each sentence. Use a dictionary to help you.**

career	salary	wage	income
pay	occupation	employment	

1 I plan to have a long *career / occupation* in advertising, but I know I will have to work hard to succeed.

2 The annual *salary / money* for this job is £35,000 a year.

3 When I first started working I used to get a weekly *pay / wage* of £20.

4 I've got a holiday job, delivering newspapers. The *salary / pay* is quite good. It's £5.00 an hour.

5 When did your *occupation / employment* with this company begin?

6 If your total annual *wage / income* is below £4,000, then you do not have to pay tax.

7 So, you would like to arrange a loan with our bank, Mr Johnson? Do you mind if I ask you a few questions first? What is your *occupation / employment*?

> **Ⓥ Vocabulary note**
>
> **career, course**
> Your **career** is the work you do over a number of years: *His acting career began when he was just 6 years old and is still going well now he is in his seventies.*
> A **course** is something you do at college or university: *I am going to do a drama course at university because I want to be an actor.*

Applying for a job

2.1 Put these in the correct order (1–7).

- Attend an interview .....
- Receive a job offer .....
- See a job advertisement ..1..
- Discuss the pay and conditions .....
- Fill in the application form .....
- Accept a job offer .....
- Start work .....

2.2 Read this job advertisement. Try to guess which words have been removed.

Southern Star Cruises

Are you free this summer? Would you like to **(1)** ....*earn*.......... some extra money? Then why not apply to join the crew of the 'Princess of the Waves', a luxury cruise ship that will be sailing round the Mediterranean this summer? We need to **(2)** .... entertainers, chefs, waiters, cleaners and sports instructors. We are looking for lively, **(3)** .... , confident individuals who will enjoy dealing with members of the public and making sure they have a fantastic holiday. Qualifications and **(4)** ....will be necessary for some of the jobs, but not for others. There are no part-time jobs, all jobs are **(5)** .... , with one day off a week. Please call 07397 783 987 and ask for an application form today. The best **(6)** .... will be called to attend an interview, which will take place between 13th and 27th April.

2.3 Now put one word from the box into each gap in the advertisement in 2.2.

candidates	employ
hard-working	experience
earn	full-time

2.4 Now complete this email with suitable words, beginning with the letter given.

Hi Dave,

Are you still looking for a **(1)** j..ob............. for the summer? If you are, you might be interested in the **(2)** a................... I saw in yesterday's paper. Southern Star Cruises are looking for people to **(3)** w.................. on a Mediterranean cruise ship called the 'Princess of the Waves'. I know you wanted a **(4)** p.................. job, but these are all full-time. I think I'll call them tomorrow and ask them to send me an **(5)** a.................. form. Would you like me to ask for one for you too? I'm going to **(6)** a.................. to be a sports instructor. I've got a life saving certificate and a teaching diploma, so I've probably got enough **(7)** q.................. , and I've got some **(8)** e.................. because I taught swimming last summer, do you remember? The **(9)** i.................. are between 13th and 27th April. It would be great fun if we went together. Let me know what you think.

Best wishes, James.

Business and industry

3.1 Ten words are hidden in this word search. Use the clues below to help you find them.

1 This person tells you what to do. b _ _ _
2 This is all the people in a company. s _ _ _ _ _
3 This person helps other people in the company. a _ _ _ _ _ _ _ _
4 This person needs to be good at typing. s _ _ _ _ _ _ _ _
5 This person works with you. c _ _ _ _ _ _ _ _
6 This person pays your wages. e _ _ _ _ _ _ _
7 This person greets people on their arrival. r _ _ _ _ _ _ _ _ _ _
8 This person works in a company. b _ _ _ _ _ _ _ _ _
9 This person runs a department. m _ _ _ _ _ _
10 This person makes big decisions about the future of the company.
   d _ _ _ _ _ _ _

R	E	C	E	P	T	I	O	N	I	S	T
A	E	O	O	E	R	P	L	S	G	E	P
T	I	L	A	T	I	O	C	S	M	C	A
H	T	L	D	I	R	E	C	T	O	R	S
U	L	E	A	H	L	E	R	A	N	E	S
L	M	A	N	A	G	E	R	F	B	T	I
B	F	G	A	T	A	R	U	F	V	A	S
O	L	U	X	S	T	I	K	O	E	R	T
S	O	E	M	P	L	O	Y	E	R	Y	A
S	T	E	R	J	I	N	E	O	P	E	N
B	U	S	I	N	E	S	S	M	A	N	T
E	G	J	E	R	T	N	L	S	A	T	Y

3.2 Match the two halves in each list to make correct phrases.

1 sign   A a conference
2 run   B an appointment
3 attend   C a business
4 cancel   D a contract
5 arrange   E a department
6 operate   F a project
7 manage   G a machine
8 lead   H a meeting

3.3 Make people and nouns from these verbs by adding –er, or –ment when possible.

arrange	employ	lead
retire	deliver	manage

3.4 Use a dictionary to check the meanings of these words and then use them to complete the sentences below.

sales figures	accounts department	customer services	in stock	business trip
brochures	on strike	company canteen	suppliers	

1 Products will be delivered immediately if they are
   ....

2 You can have lunch in the ....

3 You go on a .... to meet ....
   or customers.

4 .... are produced by the ....

5 Complaints from customers are dealt with by
   ....

6 .... show pictures of a company's
   products.

7 Workers go .... when they are unhappy.

Exam practice

SPEAKING Part 3

Look at the photos and think about how you could describe them in as much detail as you can. Now choose one photo and practise talking about it for 1 minute.

SPEAKING Part 4

When you and your partner have described your photos, the examiner will ask you to talk with your partner about the topic. Look at what the examiner says, and think about what you could say.

Examiner: *The two photos show different kinds of jobs and working environments. Now, I'd like you to talk together about the kind of jobs you do, or you would like to do.*

 20 **Now listen to two candidates interacting with one another. Notice how they ask questions and take turns to speak.**

> ### Exam Tip
> In part 4, interact with your partner! Listen and ask questions as well as speaking. Try not to talk all the time, and try not to be too quiet.

Test Four (Units 16–20)

Choose the correct letter A, B or C.

1 I've seen every single programme in The Natural World series since it started in 1985 – it's my favourite ....
  A sitcom **B** thriller **C** documentary

2 One World is a .... programme that examines what is happening on the political scene today.
  A current affairs **B** historical documentary **C** natural history

3 Let's get Dad this .... for his birthday. He's not too keen on fiction.
  A thriller **B** horror story **C** travel book

4 According to this report, a lot of people who buy best-selling books never actually .... them.
  A finish **B** end **C** complete

5 It's much cheaper to .... books from the library than it is to buy them.
  A lend **B** take **C** borrow

6 Before I buy tickets for a show I always read the .... in the newspapers to make sure it's worth seeing.
  A reviews **B** articles **C** headlines

7 I usually walk to school as the trains and buses are so .... in the morning.
  A quiet **B** crowded **C** exciting

8 The .... is much more beautiful in the countryside than in the town.
  A scenery **B** atmosphere **C** transport

9 Please tell me what the next .... says. I want to check that we are on the right road.
  A crossroads **B** signpost **C** roundabout

10 Which of the following is what is left of an ancient building?
  A ruin **B** cathedral **C** gallery

11 Where would you go if you wanted to buy medicine?
  A grocer's **B** department store **C** chemist's

12 Which of these has water coming out of it and is often found in town squares?
  A pavement **B** fountain **C** tower

13 We were sitting at the back but we could .... the actors very clearly.
  A watch **B** look **C** see

14 You must collect your tickets at least half an hour before the .... starts.
  A drama **B** theatre **C** play

15 The .... in the jazz club had an amazing keyboard technique.
   A guitarist   **B** pianist   **C** drummer

16 I'm in a drama club – I'm no good at acting but I do jobs like moving the ....
   A scenery   **B** lighting   **C** curtain

17 Harry Potter and James Bond are both very successful film ....
   A actors   **B** scenes   **C** series

18 I don't want to see a .... I prefer movies that are acted by real people.
   A cartoon   **B** comedy   **C** thriller

19 If I lose my friends in a crowded disco I often .... to find them again.
   A send a text   **B** call on the landline   **C** write an email

20 I forgot to save my work before I left the room and my little brother came and .... it all.
   A crashed   **B** emptied   **C** deleted

21 My internet connection takes ages because I have to .... it up through the telephone.
   A dial   **B** access   **C** call

22 You are not supposed to .... movies from the internet and anyway the quality is often very poor.
   A print   **B** film   **C** download

23 In this new group of houses there are several smart homes where everything is .... by computer.
   A controlled   **B** ordered   **C** produced

24 This new laptop is extremely light. It .... less than two kilos.
   A measures   **B** weighs   **C** contains

25 Which of the following jobs is a profession?
   A labourer   **B** carpenter   **C** lawyer

26 Which of these people keeps a building safe at night?
   A security guard   **B** architect   **C** builder

27 A judge .... lawyers and people who may have broken the law.
   A works for   **B** deals with   **C** looks after

28 I had a higher .... in my old job but I am much happier in my new job.
   A pay   **B** salary   **C** money

29 I applied for the job and was asked to .... an interview the following day.
   A attend   **B** receive   **C** visit

30 'Good afternoon. Could you tell me when you are going to .... the sofa I ordered from you?'
   A arrange   **B** deliver   **C** manage

Appendix 1

Phrasal verbs

Phrasal verbs have a main verb plus one or two prepositions which are part of that verb.
Sometimes the meaning of phrasal verbs is clear:

He *got down* on his knees and *picked up* the piece of paper from the floor.

Sometimes it is not so clear. Here are some phrasal verbs that you should know for PET.

break down	Our car *broke down* on the way to the airport.
break in to	Thieves *broke into* the house and stole some jewellery.
break up	Sam and Lisa have *broken up*. (*no longer married*)
	School *breaks up* next week. (*finishes for the holidays*)
bring up	The children were *brought up* to tell the truth.
call in	She *called in* to see her grandmother on the way home from work.
carry on	Everyone *carried on* working when the head teacher walked in.
come down	Digital cameras have *come down* in price. (*got cheaper*)
come on	*Come on* or we'll be late! (*Hurry up!*)
cross out	If you make a mistake, just *cross it out*.
fill in	Please *fill in* your name and address on this form.
fill up	He *filled up* the car with petrol at the garage.
find out	I'll just *find out* when the train leaves.
get along/on (with)	How does Jan *get along with* her parents in law?
get down	The reporter *got* all the details *down* in a notebook. (*wrote*)
get on with	The builders are *getting on with* the house. (*making progress*)
get on	How did you *get on* at the dentist's? (*How was it?*)
get rid of	I *got rid of* my old clothes to make room for my new ones.
give in	*Give in* your homework on Monday morning.
	Her parents *gave in* and let her have a mobile phone.
give up	After he hurt his knee, Brian had to *give up* football.
give way	In some countries you *give way* to traffic from the right. (*wait for*)
go for	The dog *went for* the postman. (*attacked*)
	Go for it! (*Do it!*)
go with	This jacket *goes with* my new trousers. (*matches*)
grow up	Joan *grew up* in Hong Kong.
hand in	He *handed* the money *in* at the police station.
hang up	He *hung up* at the end of the phone call.
hold up	Sorry I'm late – I was *held up* in the traffic. (*delayed*)
join in	Everybody *joined in* singing the song.

keep in	The children were *kept in* at break time as a punishment for behaving badly.
keep on	He *kept on* knocking but nobody came to the door.
knock out	The boxer was *knocked out* in the first round.
leave out	I *left out* the last question on the paper because I didn't have time. (*didn't do*)
look after	My mother *looks after* my baby one day a week.
look forward to	The children were all *looking forward to* the birthday party.
look out	*Look out!* There's a car coming. (*be careful*)
look up	I *looked up* the spelling in a dictionary. (*checked*)
make sure	*Make sure* that you've turned the heater off before you leave the room.
pick up	Can you *pick* me *up* on your way to college? (*give a lift*)
	I *picked up* a newspaper at the railway station. (*bought*)
plug in	The television isn't working because it's not *plugged in*!
put off	The test was *put off* until the following week as so many students were absent.
put out	*Put out* the lights when you leave.
run out of	I can only offer you black coffee as we've *run out of* milk.
set off/out	The sun was shining when they *set off* for their walk.
set up	The organisation was *set up* fifty years ago. (*started*)
sort out	I need to *sort out* these papers.
take off	The plane *took off* four hours late.
take part in	Would you like to *take part in* a quiz?
take place	It will *take place* in the school hall.
take up	She *took up* teaching as a career.
try on	Could I *try on* this pair of shoes?
throw away	Don't *throw* the newspaper *away*. I haven't read it yet.
tidy up	*Tidy up* the kitchen when you've finished cooking, please.
turn down	John asked Maria to the cinema but she *turned* him *down*. (*refused*)
wear off	The pain is *wearing off* now. (*becoming less*)
wear out	I need some new boots. This pair is *worn out*.

Appendix 2

Speaking checklist

Part 1

The examiner will ask you some simple questions about yourself, for example what you do, where you live, your likes and dislikes. You will have to spell a name, either your own or that of a town or country.

Tips

- The questions will not be difficult. Try to answer them fully.
- Avoid giving one-word answers.
- If you don't understand, ask the examiner to repeat the question.
- Relax!

Part 2

The examiner will describe a situation to you and give you a picture with some ideas to help you. You have to talk together with your partner to decide what will be the best idea for the situation.

Tips

- Make sure you understand what you have to do – you can ask the examiner to repeat the instructions.
- Take turns with your partner to discuss the ideas in the pictures.
- Try to come to an agreement with your partner at the end.

Useful phrases

What do you think about …? What about …? I think this would be good because … That's a good idea but …

Part 3

The examiner will give you a picture and ask you to talk about it on your own for about one minute.

Tips

- Try to describe the picture as fully as you can, including all the details.
- Don't worry if you don't know the word for something – try to explain it in another way.
- Keep talking until the examiner stops you.

Useful phrases

This picture shows … , It looks as if … , I think it's … because … , It makes me think of …

Part 4

This part of the test is a discussion with your partner on the same topic as the pictures you described in Part 3.

Tips

- Listen carefully so you know what the examiner wants you to talk about.
- Talk to your partner, not the examiner.
- Make sure that you and your partner take an equal part in the discussion – one partner should not say more than the other.
- Enjoy yourself!

Appendix 3

Writing checklist

In the PET exam, you need to be able to do the following things in writing:
- make arrangements and suggestions
- give information
- tell a story
- report events
- describe objects and people
- explain how you feel about things

Before you start writing

- Always read the question carefully.
  In Part 2, look for words like *suggest*, *say*, *describe*, and *apologise* which tell you what you have to do.
- Remember you only have to do **ONE** question from Part 3.
- If you choose the letter, read the question very carefully. Underline the points you have to write about. In some letters you will be giving advice and in others you will be giving information about yourself. Make sure you know what you need to do.
- Make a plan. This does not have to be long. Just spend a couple of minutes thinking about what you are going to write and make some notes. This will stop you from missing out important information. Write down any useful and relevant vocabulary that you would like to use in your answer.
- If you decide to write a story make sure it has a beginning, a middle and an end.

When you are writing

- Think about your spelling and punctuation and make sure your answer is easy to read.
- Try to use a wide range of vocabulary.
- Re-read your work as you go and do not be afraid to make changes as necessary.
- Think about the time you have available and the number of words you have been asked to write for Part 2 (35–45 words) and Part 3 (100 words). Leave enough time to complete the writing.

When you have finished writing

Re-read your work:
- to check for any spelling or punctuation errors, and
- to see if there are any places where it does not make sense or could be improved.

Appendix 4

Irregular verbs

Here is a list of irregular verb forms you should know for the PET exam.

Infinitive	Past	Past participle
be	was/were	been
become	became	become
bend	bent	bent
bite	bit	bitten
bleed	bled	bled
break	broke	broken
bring	brought	brought
build	built	built
burn	burnt/burned	burnt/burned
catch	caught	caught
choose	chose	chosen
come	came	come
cut	cut	cut
dig	dug	dug
do	did	done
drink	drank	drunk
drive	drove	driven
feel	felt	felt
fly	flew	flown
freeze	froze	frozen
get	got	got
give	gave	given
go	went	gone
grow	grew	grown
have	had	had
hide	hid	hidden
hit	hit	hit
hold	held	held
keep	kept	kept
kneel	knelt	knelt
know	knew	known
lay	laid	laid
lead	led	led
leave	left	left
lend	lent	lent
let	let	let
lie	lay	lain
light	lit	lit
make	made	made
mean	meant	meant
meet	met	met

Infinitive	Past	Past participle
pay	paid	paid
put	put	put
read	read	read
ride	rode	ridden
ring	rang	rung
rise	rose	risen
run	ran	run
say	said	said
see	saw	seen
sell	sold	sold
send	sent	sent
set	set	set
shake	shook	shaken
shine	shone	shone
shoot	shot	shot
shut	shut	shut
sing	sang	sung
sink	sank	sunk
sit	sat	sat
sleep	slept	slept
speak	spoke	spoken
spend	spent	spent
stand	stood	stood
steal	stole	stolen
stick	stuck	stuck
strike	struck	struck
sweep	swept	swept
swim	swam	swum
swing	swung	swung
take	took	taken
teach	taught	taught
tear	tore	torn
tell	told	told
think	thought	thought
throw	threw	threw
wake	woke	woken
wear	wore	worn
win	won	won
wind	wound	wound
write	wrote	written

Appendix 5

Glossary

If you find a word you don't know in the instructions to the exercises in this book you can check the meaning here.

adjective
describes a noun
a **big** house
The bride looked **beautiful**.

adverb
describes a verb
She walks **quickly**.
or an adjective
a **very** clever boy

compound words
are formed from more than one word
a **desktop** computer, a **dishwasher**

confuse
think one thing is another
Don't **confuse** these two words.

definition
an explanation of the meaning
The dictionary will give you a **definition** of this word.

error
a mistake
This book will warn you about common **errors**.

infinitive
the basic form of a verb, often used with 'to'
Can I **go** home now?
I'd like **to go** home now.

-ing form of the verb
in continuous tenses
It's **raining**.
used like a noun
Singing is fun.
or an adjective
an **exciting** book

noun
a word that refers to a person, place, object, idea, or feeling
dog, information, rice

phrase
a group of words that go together
on business
by all means

phrasal verb
a main verb plus one or two prepositions
Sometimes the meaning of phrasal verbs is clear:
Mary **looked at** the picture.
Sometimes the meaning is not so clear.
Can you **look after** Lucy this afternoon?

preposition
a word like off, into, on which is often followed by a pronoun or a noun

refer to / reference
look for information in
Please **refer to** the appendix for a list of verbs.
A dictionary is a **reference** book.

task
something you have to do
In the speaking test, one of the **tasks** is to describe a picture.

verb
describes what is happening
She **walks** quickly.
The bride **looked** beautiful.

Recording script

Recording 1

Stan: We have to decide what to do for our holiday this year!

Julie: I think we should go on a cruise. Don't you think it would be wonderful to have a holiday on a ship, sailing across the ocean and calling at a different port each day?

Stan: That does sound fantastic but isn't it expensive?

Julie: It's not as much as you think. Look, in this brochure there's a cruise to the Mediterranean that's only £500 per person.

Stan: Oh yes. It goes to Italy, then the Greek islands, Turkey, and finishes in Egypt. Oh, it looks great.

Julie: It does, except that we've been to a couple of those places already.

Stan: You're right. That wouldn't be very exciting. What about this one, to Canada and the Arctic? Look at the amazing scenery, all these mountains, and ice for miles!

Julie: We've only got a week, remember. We need something that's a bit nearer.

Stan: OK. What about this one in Northern Europe? It starts in Poland and then goes to Sweden. After that, Germany and then Denmark.

Julie: That's a possibility. There's another one here that goes to Norway, Denmark and the Netherlands. It's the same number of days, but you spend more time on the ship and less time visiting cities.

Stan: That sounds more relaxing, doesn't it? And look at these photos of the ship!

Julie: It's very smart, isn't it?

Stan: Yes, and read this list of activities. I don't think you could ever be bored on this ship.

Julie: I see what you mean. It's a pity there's no indoor pool though. I love swimming and it will be too cold for us to swim in the sea.

Stan: It certainly will! So do you want to book it?

Julie: OK. Let's try it! If we like it, we can do a longer cruise next year – maybe South America, or Africa or India!

Stan: Or maybe the whole world!

Recording 2

1 Lawyer: I love my job, but it can be very tiring. I work long hours and I have to look smart all the time. I do love my suits – they are all very fashionable and expensive. The only trouble is, in my company we all look the same – it's a bit like wearing a uniform, and there are days when I don't feel like putting one on, or wearing any make-up, but I know I have to, especially if I'm going to be in court that day. I don't think the judge would be very happy if I arrived wearing a tracksuit and trainers!

2 Lifeguard: People think I have an easy job. Lots of my friends are very jealous. They say I just have to stand around all day in a swimming costume, looking good. Of course that's not true, I'm responsible for the safety of this whole area, so I have to concentrate hard. I can't relax for a minute. Also, this job is not very good for your looks. We all wear the same red T shirt and shorts,

which are not very stylish and I have to wear a hat and lots of sun cream every day, otherwise I would get badly burnt.

3 Actor: When I was in my twenties I was very good looking and I used to get great parts. I remember in one play I wore the most beautiful long silk dresses, there were about 10 of them in total. Luckily they were quite loose because sometimes I only had 2 minutes to take one dress off and put another one on, before I had to go back out on stage. Now, things are a bit different. I generally play middle-aged women dressed in woollen skirts and sweaters and flat shoes, the kind of clothes I wear in real life! I still have to get in and out of them in 2 minutes though!

4 Fashion model: There is a lot of travelling involved in my job and I spend quite a lot of time in hotels, so I buy clothes that don't need much ironing when you take them out of the suitcase. I don't own that many clothes, which you might find surprising. My jeans are my favourite things – I wear them all the time. Of course when I'm working I wear the most fantastic things, designed by the top people in the business, but to be honest most of them are not very comfortable, and not my style.

Recording 3

Ali: Hi, Nick.

Nick: Oh, hi, Ali.

Ali: How did you get on helping at the holiday camp? Did the children enjoy it or were they all homesick?

Nick: Well I must admit some of the younger kids were a little bit unhappy because they'd never been away on their own before and didn't know some of the other kids. But they soon recovered. By the last day they didn't want to go home they were having such a great time.

Ali: What sort of things did you do with them?

Nick: Well there were some trips, including a visit to Hardwick Castle. I think they were expecting it to be rather boring, especially when they heard they were having a guided tour. But they were wrong – the guide was very entertaining. He told them some interesting stories and really made the history of the castle come alive. They loved it, especially the prisons down in the cellars.

Ali: I can imagine – what sort of sports activities did they do?

Nick: Well, there was sailing and windsurfing, and horse-riding. That was a great success. None of the kids had ridden before and some were a bit worried about being near the horses . One boy called Sam kept falling off at first, but he became a really good rider – now he's asked his parents to buy him a pony for his birthday!

Ali: I wonder if they know how much it costs to keep a horse! How about the sailing? Did anyone fall in?

Nick: Luckily no, though a girl called Tara decided to jump into the swimming pool with all her clothes on – she's usually very responsible. I don't know what made her do such a stupid thing. Of course all her new friends thought it was really funny. Fortunately she could swim.

Ali: So at least you didn't have to go and rescue her.

Nick: That's true. We finished up with a barbecue on the last evening with singing and dancing and some fireworks – that was great fun, the kids enjoyed it enormously. They were all promising to keep in touch with each other and come again next year.

Ali: Oh well it sounds as if you had a good time too, will you be going back next year?

Nick: Yes, definitely. I love working with kids!

Recording 4a

Laura: We've recently moved into a new house with my parents. Mum has always looked after Bella while I'm at work. I used to get up at 5am to get Bella ready to take her to Mum's house. Now we all live together. We get on really well with each other and Bella looks forward to being with her Grandma every day.

Ros: Dad thinks I'm still a child. He won't even let me go out with my friends at weekends. Once I was really looking forward to going to a party. Mum had said it was OK but he said I was too young to be out in the evening and kept me in. He doesn't realise that teenagers need more independence when they're growing up.

John: After my grandmother, died my grandfather moved in with us so my mother could look after him. Grandad and I didn't get along at all. He kept on complaining about my clothes, my hair, my music, even my girlfriend. I'm sure it was difficult for my parents bringing up a teenager. I used to go out with my mates as often as I could.

Recording 4b

Interviewer: Andrew, tell us about 'The week the women went'.

Andrew: Well, it was an experiment to see how the men in the village would manage if their women all went away on holiday for a week. The television company wanted to see if the men could look after their families and join in village life in the same way that their wives do.

Interviewer: Your sons are 10 and 13 – how did they feel when your wife left for the week?

Andrew: Very upset. We started by planning our menu. They wanted their favourite meals, but when we looked them up in the recipe book they were far too complicated to make. So we got lots of ready meals from the supermarket. Kim, my wife, never usually buys them because they're expensive.

Interviewer: Did you get together with the other men?

Andrew: Oh yes. There was a social evening for all the dads so I got a baby-sitter to look after the boys – normally Kim would do that. I hadn't expected to see the men introducing themselves to each other – I thought they were all friends already.

Interviewer: Do you think your relationship with your sons changed while Kim was away?

Andrew: Definitely. We made a big effort to communicate with each other. The older son had some problems at school, which normally Kim sorts out, so I was pleased I could help him. Also we chatted about different things – sport for example, and less about people and shopping.

Interviewer: You must have been looking forward to seeing Kim at the end of the week.

Andrew: I'll say. The boys had baked her a cake and I'd got her some flowers. She was really delighted but she noticed that they were wearing the same clothes as when she left! I'm afraid I hadn't done any washing!

Interviewer: And what about the village – has life changed at all as a result of the programme?

Andrew: A lot of people want to move here, but there aren't any houses for sale. Several husbands offered to give up their jobs to look after their families full-time. Of course that didn't last long! Before the project most of us men had never spent 24 hours with our children and the village was just a place to eat and sleep. Now we are all friends and keen to do things together to make living here even better. It's been a very positive experience.

Interviewer: Andrew, that's great. Thank you for talking to us.

Recording 5

When I was a young child we lived in a flat near the city centre. It was really convenient and we had some fantastic neighbours. Then my dad decided he wanted to move out of the city, so he bought this place. We've been living here ever since. My Dad loves it because it's so peaceful and beautiful, and he's right, the views are wonderful. But mum and I miss the town. It's too quiet for us here – we'd prefer to be somewhere a bit more lively. In fact, we've found a house that would be perfect. It hasn't got much of a garden but it has got a garage. It doesn't look very big from the outside but it has got lots of rooms inside, including a basement. The best thing about it is that it's just a short walk to the centre of town. The only thing we have to do now is persuade Dad to buy it!

Recording 6

1

Male: Let's plant a tree in the back garden. It will be great for wildlife and it will give us some shade in the summer.

Female: Oh I don't know. Won't it be expensive, and a lot of hard work?

Male: Not really. I'll do all the digging. It'll look great when it's done, trust me. You're always talking about ways to help the environment – well, this is a really good way to start.

Female: Oh, OK, then. What kind of tree shall we get?

2

Male: What are you going to do about your car? It broke down again yesterday, didn't it?

Female: Yes. I'm not sure what to do. I could sell it and buy a bike. Or I could try and fix it one more time.

Male: You know it will only break down again. It always does!

Female: You're right. I'll sell it. That way I'll get fit and help the environment at the same time!

3

Male: I went to the bottle bank today, and guess what. It was completely full!

Female: Oh that's a shame. Did you have to bring all the glass home again?

Male: Yes. There was a sign saying not to leave anything on the ground. I really don't understand why they can't empty it more often. What's the point of having a bottle bank if you can't put any bottles into it?

Female: You're right. Maybe you should write a letter.

4

Female: I think nuclear power stations are the best way to make energy because they don't make any pollution.

Male: That's not true. Just think about the waste they produce. Some of it is dangerous for thousands of years.

Female: There are safe ways to store it now – they can bury it deep under the ground.

Male: Well I don't think that's safe – I would like to see more electricity being made from wind and the sun.

5

Male: Did you get that book about the environment I asked you to buy for me?

Female: Oh, sorry. I completely forgot. What's it called?

Male: How to Save the Planet. It costs £8.99 and you can get it from Wetherby's bookshop.

Female: OK, I'll get it for you tomorrow when I go to town.

Recording 7a

Presenter: I'm in the Bluewater shopping centre to find out about young people's shopping habits. I spoke first to Dario, who's a computer programmer. Dario, are you enjoying yourself?

Dario: Not really, to be quite honest. My girlfriend persuaded me I needed some new shoes. I've been to lots of shops and tried on dozens of shoes but I didn't like any of them. At least I got some CDs so it hasn't been a complete waste of time. It'll be a long time before I come shopping here again though.

Presenter: Now let's hear from Margot, a student from London.

Margot: I love to come here with my friends in the holidays. I check out the latest fashions in magazines and on the store websites before I come. So far today I've bought a jacket, a hat, some earrings and a book for a friend – but it's all with my birthday money. I find shopping for clothes really exciting. I'd like a credit card but I can't get one until I'm 18. I think I'm sensible with money.

Presenter: Next I spoke to Jennie who's 15 and still at school. Jennie, you enjoy shopping after school and at weekends and you say you've bought a dress and a matching handbag. Do you think you're a sensible shopper like Margot?

Jennie: Well, I must admit that I sometimes buy clothes without trying them on, just because they're cheap. Then when I get home I find they don't fit or I don't like them any more. But I never take them back for a refund or an exchange. I've got quite a few jumpers and skirts in my cupboard that I've never worn – I suppose it's a waste of my pocket money really. But I've tried this dress on. It's half price and it fits perfectly so I know I'll wear it.

Recording 7b

This looks like a dress shop. I think the woman on the left is the customer and she has just bought something because there is a bag on the table where you pay and she is giving some money to the other woman. She must be the shop assistant. I'm not sure what it's called in English, but behind her there's a, hmm, sort of computer where you put the money – and on the left there are lots of blouses and T-shirts hanging up and on the other side there are some jackets. The woman on the left has got short hair and big silver earrings. The shop assistant has got long hair and she looks very friendly because she is smiling. I think this looks like a very nice shop, and I'd like to go there.

Recording 8

1   What does the man choose for dessert?

Waitress: Can I interest you in a dessert, sir? We've got some lovely strawberries, they were only picked this morning. Chef has made them into a beautiful cheese cake – or you can have them on their own with ice cream.

Man: I don't really want anything sweet – have you got cheese and biscuits?

Waitress: I'm terribly sorry sir, there's no cheese left. We're waiting for some more to be delivered.

Man: In that case I'll have the fruit as it's so fresh, but without any ice cream. The first course was very filling.

Waitress: Certainly, sir …

2   What does the woman's rice dish contain?

I hope you like your rice cooked this way – I usually make it with chicken and mushrooms, and add some cream at the end but this time I've decided to try a recipe I saw on the television – it still has the mushrooms and all the other ingredients, but it uses seafood instead of chicken and I've replaced the cream with lemon – so it'll be much healthier!

3   What will Sam's mother do on his birthday?

Mother: Sam, how about if we all go to the new Chinese restaurant on your birthday? Or would you like me to cook your favourite meal here?

Sam: I don't know Mum – I'm so slow with chopsticks. Anyway, Sally's promised to cook a meal at her house for me and a few classmates.

Mother: Oh, I didn't realise you'd already got something arranged – why don't I bake a carrot cake for you to take to Sally's for dessert?

Sam: That'd be great Mum. Maybe we can go to the Chinese restaurant some other time.

Recording 9a

Announcement A

Great Northern Railways would like to apologise for the delays to today's services. These have been caused by a lack of staff at some stations. Information about the new times of all arrivals and departures will be displayed on the boards which can be found on the platform, waiting room and main hall of the station. We are hoping to have this information ready to give you in 20 minutes. We have not cancelled any services today, but you may have to wait up to 40 minutes for your train. If you wish to make other arrangements for your journey today, and would like your money back, please see staff in the ticket office who will give you a refund. We would ask you to be patient as this may take some time. Thank you for your attention.

Announcement B

This is an announcement for all passengers travelling on flight 397 to Budapest. This flight has been cancelled due to bad weather. The forecast for tomorrow is better and there are two flights to Budapest tomorrow morning, one at 8.00 am and one at 9.00 am. We will make sure that all passengers booked on flight 397 will travel to Budapest on one of these flights. Could all passengers please remain here in the departure lounge until your details have been taken. We will then take you to a hotel where you will spend the night. The cost of all accommodation and meals will be paid for by the airline. We would like to apologise for any inconvenience caused.

Recording 9b

Man: On today's programme I'm going to be talking about the famous Icehotel at Jukkasjarvi in Sweden. Every year a team of builders and artists from all over the world come to the little village of Jukkasjarvi and build a hotel out of snow and ice. In the spring it melts and the next year they start all over again. The hotel, which is inside the Arctic Circle is just a short drive from the airport, and is suitable for most people except families with very young children. Jukkasjarvi has a small museum and a pretty church but not much else, so evenings are usually spent in the Icehotel, having a drink in the bar and admiring the building. The ice used to build the hotel is amazingly clear. When you open the doors and enter the hotel, the sight of this ice, with the light shining through it, is just fantastic. In late December and early January ice rooms will be ready for guests but other parts of the hotel will be unfinished. If you come at this time you will be able to watch the artists making their sculptures. If you prefer to see the hotel once everything is completed then the best time to travel is from the middle of January. Various activities are organised for guests at the Icehotel. There are guided tours of the hotel in English and Swedish at various times of the day where you can learn about the history of this fantastic place. You will also have the chance to make your own ice-sculpture. Classes are at 11 am daily. The hotel provides all the ice and tools you need and hot drinks – you just bring your ideas. There are also two different trips, both quite reasonably priced. One is a climbing trip to the top of Mount Puimonen from where there are wonderful views of the Icehotel. The other is a 5km cross country skiing trip. A driver takes you out and then you ski back to the hotel. It is a good idea to book these activities at least three weeks before your arrival as they fill up quickly.

There is some heated accommodation at the hotel and if you are worried that sleeping in an ice room will not suit you, you can reserve one of the heated rooms at extra cost. You can of course spend all your nights in heated accommodation and not take the ice room at all, but in my opinion, this would be a shame.

Recording 10a

Speaker 1: Before you set out it's essential to check the weather forecast. Then you should arrive at the festival campsite early to get a good place for your tent – fairly close to the car park for carrying your bags but also not too far from the main festival area. Don't forget a raincoat, strong shoes and a pocket light. Finding your tent in a dark rainy campsite after a night's dancing can be difficult.

Speaker 2: I joined a club when I was at university and enjoyed going away for weekends. The weather can be changeable so comfortable, waterproof clothes plus the proper boots and a helmet are essential. All your safety equipment should be good quality. The best part about it for me is the feeling you get when you make it to the top of a steep cliff and see the ground a long, long way below.

Speaker 3: We always start with a 45-minute beginner's lesson. You don't need a special costume, just soft shoes and comfortable clothes. Each week we learn a series of four new movements that join together to make a short routine. After that there's a 30-minute freestyle period when you can practise what you've just learnt. There's no need to be shy – you can ask anyone you like onto the floor – no-one ever refuses and the DJ plays some great music.

Speaker 4: You must have sensible footwear and a life jacket. The water can be very cold all year round so a wetsuit is most important. Getting started needn't be expensive if you join a club. You might even be invited to be a crew member on someone else's boat. Unlike some sports, you don't have to give up as you get older and it's something the whole family can enjoy together – I started at the age of six and my grandfather still comes out with me.

Recording 10b

Female: Shall I start? What do you think about going to the gym?

Male: Well it's OK but it's quite expensive. Maybe our friend can't afford it. And it's not easy to chat when you're exercising. I think going to this club is better. What do you think?

Female: I agree, because you can play table tennis there and dance and it's fun. Getting a dog is good too – our friend can take it for walks and meet people in the park.

Male: That's a good idea, but when he goes on holiday somebody has to look after it and food for dogs is expensive. This one's good – learning to play the guitar.

Female: Do you think so? I don't agree. He'll only meet his teacher.

Male: Yes, but if he can play the guitar he can join a band and make lots of friends that way. Or what about this one – in a theatre helping with a play. I think that would be a really good way to meet people.

Female: Yes, he likes acting. So I think that's best.

Male: Or going to the club, that's good as well.

Recording 11

I'm afraid I don't have very good memories of my school days. I think teachers were very strict in those days, much stricter than they are now. When I listen to my grandchildren talking about school, I think it sounds more like a holiday camp. We had so many rules to think about all the time. It was an all girls school and we had to wear this awful uniform. It was grey and yellow and so uncomfortable. And you had to have it just right. If one button was wrongly fastened, or your tie was too loose, you were punished straight away. We also had to be on time every day, if we were late we got into terrible trouble. Teachers weren't afraid of shouting at you or even hitting you in those days! And of course, we always had to talk nicely to the teachers and never be rude. They weren't very worried about us getting qualifications though. They thought we would all just get married after school and that we didn't need careers or university.

I was always very well-behaved and tried to stay out of trouble as much as possible. But I do remember making one teacher very angry once. I had been absent from school for a few days because I had been ill, and it was my first day back. I was in my geography lesson and the teacher asked everyone to hand in their homework. Of course I hadn't done it because I had been away and that was fine, the teacher knew that. But then my friend asked me about my illness and I started telling her all about it. When the teacher saw me, he got very angry. I thought he would make me write lines – you know 'I must not talk in class' 100 times, or stay behind after school. But in the end I had to spend my whole lunchtime collecting litter from the playground – what a horrible punishment. Anyway, it worked because I don't think I ever chatted in class again!

Recording 12

Patient A

Doctor: Have a seat Miss Brown. How can I help?

Miss B: I'm afraid I've got terrible earache.

Doctor: I see. Is it on both sides?

Miss B: No, it's just the left one.

Doctor: Right, well I'd better examine it. Hmm, well there's nothing there, your ear looks quite healthy. Have you got a sore throat Miss Brown?

Miss B: Well, yes, a bit.

Doctor: Let me have a look at your throat – open wide and say 'Ah'.

Miss B: Aaah.

Doctor: Oh yes. You'd better see a dentist – there might be a problem with the tooth at the back on that side.

Miss B: Oh right, I'll make an appointment straight away. I have had toothache recently.

Doctor: And I'll give you a prescription for some tablets for the pain. You can get them at the chemist's.

Miss B: I will, thank you very much.

Patient B

Doctor: Oh dear Will, what's happened to you!

Will: I was playing football and I got kicked. My leg really hurts. I hope it's not broken.

Doctor: Let me examine it. Hmmm. Can you put your weight on it?

Will: Hmm. Ow, no, it's too painful!

Doctor: OK, now can you bend your knee?

Will: Yes, that's not a problem. But I can't move my ankle at all.

Doctor: I don't think it's broken but you'd better go to hospital for an x-ray to make sure. I'll call an ambulance to take you there.

Will: So will I be able to play in the football match next week?

Doctor: I doubt it very much. Even if it's not broken, you'll still have to rest your leg for at least 3 weeks to let it recover.

Will: Oh. Thank you doctor.

Patient C

Doctor: Hello, come and sit down. What can I do for you?

Mother: My little boy's cut his hand. I was getting dinner ready and somehow he picked up the knife when my back was turned. There was a lot of blood. I tried to put a plaster on it but ...

Doctor: Lets have a look ... Yes, he's got a cut on his thumb. It's not too bad. It's stopped bleeding now. I'll put a dressing on it and nice big bandage and he'll be fine.

Mother: Oh thank you very much doctor.

Doctor: No problem.

Recording 13

Announcer: And now here is Carol Johnson the organiser of this year's Abington Fun Run.

Carol: Thank you. Yes, I'm delighted to be able to tell you that this year the Abington Fun Run will be at 11 am, on Sunday May 24th, so make a note in your diary. It's open to runners of any age and ability – children, their parents, grandparents, friends, couples or single runners and it's an excellent opportunity to get out into the fresh air for some exercise.

The course of the fun run will be through the beautiful environment of Abington Park and the total distance will be 3 kilometres, starting and finishing at the football ground. That's on the south side of the park, very close to the main entrance.

Runners will be able to use the changing rooms in the Hockey Club. These are near the starting point for the run and are very big with excellent showers. There is also a large car park outside for those of you who need it.

Abington Fun Run is a race in which there are no winners or losers. Everyone who takes part will be given something to remember the day by. Last year it was a T-shirt. This year it will be a water bottle so it's certain to be very useful.

The cost for adults is £8 if you register in advance or £10 on the day. Any child under the age of 15 can take part free but there's a lower age limit of eight.

If you would like to join in the fun run, entry forms and an information pack with lots of useful tips for improving your fitness and preparing for the run are available from any newsagent or you can download one from the sports development website at www. funrun.org. See you there!

Recording 14a

1 Which photograph are they looking at?

Female: Can I see that photo, James? Is this where you went on holiday?

Male: That's right. Our hotel was in a beautiful valley about 25 miles from the coast, but we drove to this beach every day. We used to go for long walks on the cliff paths. There were lots of climbers there, it was quite exciting to watch them.

Female: And are you going to go back there next year?

Male: We might, but we're thinking of going to Indonesia to visit the rainforest. My wife loves animals and wants to see the wildlife there!

2 Where is Jim's house?

Male: Hi Sue, it's Jim here. I'm really pleased you are coming to my party on Saturday. I'm just giving you a quick call to give you directions as I know you've never been here before. The best way to come is straight down the A347. You'll pass the lake and then you will see a small wood on your left. After you have passed that, you come round a very steep hill. Then you'll see a big hotel and my house is opposite that. OK, see you Saturday.

3 Which pets does Tony have?

Female: Hello Tony, is this your new dog? He's lovely! How does he get on with the rest of your pets?

Male: He loves the cat – they're best friends. But he's not so sure about the parrot – he finds her a bit frightening!

Female: And what about your snake?

Male: Oh, I had to sell him. He got too big for me to look after properly. So I got a fish to go in the space where he was.

Recording 14b

Man: Welldean Wild Animal Park is open 7 days a week, every day of the year. Between April and September, we are open 10am until 6pm, and from October to March we are open 10am to 4pm. Last admission will be one hour before closing time.

We have a wide range of wild animals for you to see, including monkeys, Asian elephants, African lions and a special kind of camel which has almost disappeared in the wild now. All the animals live in environments which are as similar to their natural habitats as possible.

Our newest arrival is a brown bear. This animal comes from south and eastern Europe and parts of Asia. It lives in forests and eats many different things, including fruit and nuts, roots, grasses and insects. It will also eat fish and small animals such as rabbits if they are available.

The animals at Welldean wander freely around the park. Therefore, for your own safely, we ask you to stay in your car as you drive through the park, and to keep your windows closed at all times. Refreshments are available at several locations. The Café on the Lake is a restaurant serving hot meals and a variety of children's meals. The Café on the Hill serves fast food such as burgers and sandwiches. There are also several kiosks and vending machines around the park.

If you would like to support our work, you can get involved by joining our Animal Club or by adopting an animal. It costs £12.50 a year to join the club. You will get a newsletter every month. Adopting an animal costs between £10 and £200 depending on the animal. Call 02785 453 7865 for more information.

We look forward to seeing you at Welldean Wild Animal Park and hope you will enjoy your visit.

Recording 15a

On Wednesday we can expect a quite a few showers across most of the United Kingdom, and in Scotland we may see some heavy rain, which could last for several hours in some places. Temperatures will remain low everywhere. By evening the rain will disappear but the clear skies mean that on Wednesday night a widespread frost will develop, with the possibility of fog appearing in river valleys. There will be a lot of bright sunshine around again on Thursday, with light winds, but it will get a little cloudier later on in the day. This cloud will not be heavy enough to produce any rain, however. Friday will be another beautiful day, again with a lot of sun around, but there is the chance of some snow falling on higher ground.

Recording 15b

Male: What do you think about this idea? They could stay inside by the fire. But I think that's very boring. Do you agree?

Female: Yes I do. Maybe they can go for a walk in the countryside? What do you think?

Male: That sounds fun, but it might be wet and dirty there. They'll need some boots. What about doing something indoors, like visiting a museum? It's nice and warm in there.

Female: You're right. I don't think fishing is very good in the winter.

Male: Neither do I, it's much too cold. But what about going ice-skating?

Female: That's a good idea. Maybe they can borrow some skating boots.

Male: Yes. It'll be really fun and maybe afterwards they could go and have coffee and a cake together. What do you think?

Female: Yes, I agree.

Recording 16

Ruby: Hi Federico, – our English teacher's given us this questionnaire about people's reading habits. Would you mind answering some questions?

Federico: OK, Ruby.

Ruby: Well my first question is: when do you read? For example I generally read before I go to sleep at night or if I wake up early in the morning. How about you?

Federico: I fall asleep as soon as my head touches the pillow and I never have time in the morning. To be honest I don't have a set time or place for reading – but I like to read when I'm travelling – on the bus or the train, or on a plane. It helps to pass the time.

Ruby: Sure. How many hours a week do you spend reading?

Federico: Well it varies, but half an hour on the bus, 5 days a week – plus maybe another half hour, so about 3 hours in total.

Ruby: I probably read more than you – more like 4 hours. Now this is the interesting bit – what sort of books do you like? Hmm … Science fiction, horror stories, books about war?

Federico: I've read all the Harry Potter books so you could say I like fantasy novels. But really I prefer travel books and biographies. I think you can learn a lot from non-fiction, don't you?

Ruby: I suppose so, but I learn enough facts at school. In general I prefer to read something light in my free time.

Federico: What, love stories and murder mysteries?

Ruby: Exactly, fiction's perfect for relaxing – don't you agree?

Federico: I'm afraid I think those sort of books are a bit of a waste of time.

Ruby: OK. Last question. What was the last book you read?

Federico: The title was Planets at War. It was science fiction. Would you like to borrow it?

Ruby: No it's OK thanks – I've just finished a thriller called 'Murder in the dark' and now I must get on with some schoolwork. At least I've finished my questionnaire. Thanks for your help Federico!

Recording 17

There are about 60,000 people in my town, so it's quite large. It's an ancient town and luckily it's been well looked after, so it looks good, especially the old square in the town centre which is famous for its 500 year-old houses. We don't have trams or underground trains, but there is an excellent bus service. I never have to wait long for one and they are not too expensive. There are even night buses, which is great because I love going out in the evenings. My town has a good range of restaurants, bars and nightclubs and in fact people come from quite far away to go to them. We've also got an arts centre, where you can see plays, films and exhibitions of paintings and sculpture. The old theatre and 2 cinemas closed down recently so we are lucky to have these new ones, and all under one roof, which is great. There is also a museum which I've been to with school a few times. It is quite interesting because the Romans used to live here, so there are some nice things to look at. I am more interested in sport though, especially swimming. There is a leisure centre in town, but it doesn't have a gym and the pool is tiny. Also my brother is always complaining that there is nowhere to play football. We do have some lovely parks and open spaces but none of them have football pitches in them. That's one thing I would like to improve about my town.

Recording 18

And now it's time to find out what's on at the Arts Centre.

The week's entertainment starts on Monday with a play based on the novel 'Birds on the wing' by author Philip Cruise. Set on a Greek island in the last century it tells a story of true love that succeeds in the face of great difficulties.

Tuesday brings a salsa workshop, led by Diana Fransen. This exciting new mix of exercise and dance, accompanied by Latin American music, is great fun. The two hours will be over before you realise it.

There are only places for 20 people so book now if you're interested. The Matsuri drummers from Japan come to the Arts Centre on Wednesday. If you think drumming is just a lot of loud noise think again – their costumes and lighting effects are amazing.

On Thursday Highgate's own Silver Band, directed by Leslie Ager, perform a concert of popular classical pieces. There will be a chance for the audience to request their favourite tunes.

The jazz singer and guitarist, Maddie Felix, visits Highgate on Friday evening as part of her concert tour to celebrate her new CD. There are still a few tickets left for this gig, but hurry, they are selling out fast.

Our regular series of Saturday afternoon films for all the family continues with Beauty and the Beast, a musical based on the traditional French story. This film is suitable for anyone over 5 years old and will be shown at 3:15 and 6:15.

To book tickets for any of these events, phone the box office on 714170, or check out the website.

And even if you don't come to one of these performances, why not enjoy a coffee in the Arts Centre coffee shop and look at this week's exhibition of sea pictures, painted by members of the Highgate art group in our coffee shop gallery – you may even decide to buy one.

Recording 19a

Eva: Carl, How long do you spend on your computer each evening?

Carl: Well my college work usually takes at least two hours.

Eva: Is that all? I think maybe I spend too long looking for information – I start off by researching one topic on a website and then I follow a link to something else. Suddenly I realise how late it is and I'm on a completely different subject and I still haven't finished the work I was supposed to do.

Carl: You can waste a lot of time surfing the internet and following links to other websites.

Eva: The trouble is I find it so fascinating.

Carl: But you do know that you can't believe everything you read on the internet, don't you Eva?

Eva: Oh yes, that's why I never go in chat rooms – you have no idea who you're talking to and what they might find out about you.

Carl: Chat rooms are OK so long as you're sensible and don't give out any personal information. I go in some music chatrooms from time to time, not very often. I talk to friends there. I download quite a lot of music from the internet too, usually while I'm doing my homework. And I've got several friends in different countries who I keep in touch with by email.

Eva: Me too, and that takes up a lot of time.

Carl: What I really like are computer games, especially the ones you can play against other people online. Sometimes I stay up really late playing.

Eva: I find them boring and it's not good for you to sit in front of a screen for too long. That's what I'm worried about.

Carl: You're right. I tell you what –I'll try to limit my time playing online games if you stop surfing websites that aren't going to be useful for your work.

Eva: OK, that's a good idea, and then let's go to the cinema one evening with the time that we've saved.

Carl: Great!

Recording 19b

Introducing the brand new Lapbook, the latest in our family of high-speed, affordable, space-saving laptop computers. Its extra bright screen is 32.5 cm wide and the Lapbook is only 2.75 cm thick so you can take this little machine anywhere. It won't weigh you down either – the new Lapbook weighs only 2.36 kilos thanks to its lightweight plastic case.

The Lapbook is a powerful machine with 512 megabytes of memory and a 60 gigabyte hard drive. And as far as speed is concerned, at 5,400 rpm, the Lapbook is even faster than any previous laptop computers.

At only £637.45, or £749.50 including tax, the Lapbook is the perfect present for yourself or your family. Available from all good computer stores now.

Recording 20

Candidate 1: Do you have a job?

Candidate 2: Yes, I work as a computer programmer in a bank. Hmm … What about you?

Candidate 1: I'm a student. I'm studying to become an architect.

Candidate 2: Ahh … That's interesting. Are you enjoying the course?

Candidate 1: I am but it's very difficult. And I have heard that it might be difficult to get a job afterwards, because there are not many jobs for architects at the moment.

Candidate 2: But it's a good career if you can be successful. Ahh … There are quite a few famous architects.

Candidate 1: I suppose so. Hmm … Do you like being a computer programmer?

Candidate 2: It's OK but I find it a bit boring sometimes. I don't like being in an office all day, and sitting in front of a screen for hours and hours is not very good for my eyes. I may change my job in a few years.

Candidate 1: Oh. What do you think you will do?

Candidate 2: I'd like to have a job in the countryside. I might buy a small farm and keep animals. I won't earn as much money but I think it would be more enjoyable.

Wordlist

UNIT 1

CONTINENTS AND REGIONS
Africa /ˈæfrɪkə/
Asia /ˈeɪʒə/
Australia /ɒsˈtreɪliə/
Europe /ˈjʊərəp/
North America /nɔːθ əˈmerɪkə/
South America /saʊθ əˈmerɪkə/
The Arctic /ði ˈɑːktɪk/
The Mediterranean /ðə ˌmedɪtərˈeɪniən/

COUNTRIES
Argentina /ˌɑːdʒənˈtiːnə/
Austria /ˈɒstriə/
Brazil /brəˈzɪl/
Canada /ˈkænədə/
China /ˈtʃaɪnə/
Denmark /ˈdenmɑːk/
Ecuador /ˈekwədɔː/
Egypt /ˈiːdʒɪpt/
France /frɑːns/
Germany /ˈdʒɜːməni/
Greece /griːs/
India /ˈɪndiə/
Italy /ˈɪtəli/
Japan /dʒəˈpæn/
Kenya /ˈkenjə/
Korea /kəˈriːə/
Mexico /ˈmeksɪkəʊ/
Morocco /məˈrɒkəʊ/
Norway /ˈnɔːweɪ/
Poland /ˈpəʊlənd/
Portugal /ˈpɔːtʃəgəl/
Russia /ˈrʌʃə/
Spain /speɪn/
Sweden /ˈswiːdən/
Switzerland /ˈswɪtsələnd/
Thailand /ˈtaɪlænd/
The Netherlands /ðə ˈneðələndz/
The USA /ðə ˌjuːesˈeɪ/
Turkey /ˈtɜːki/
Venezuela /ˌvenɪˈzweɪlə/
Zambia /ˈzæmbiə/

LANGUAGES / NATIONALITIES
American /əˈmerɪkən/
Arabic /ˈærəbɪk/
Canadian /kəˈneɪdiən/
Danish /ˈdeɪnɪʃ/
English /ˈɪŋglɪʃ/
French /frentʃ/
German /ˈdʒɜːmən/
Italian /ɪˈtæliən/
Japanese /ˌdʒæpənˈiːz/
Polish /ˈpəʊlɪʃ/
Portuguese /ˌpɔːtʃəˈgiːz/
Russian /ˈrʌʃən/
Spanish /ˈspænɪʃ/
Swedish /ˈswiːdɪʃ/
Swiss /swɪs/

GEOGRAPHY

Nouns
bay /beɪ/
border /ˈbɔːdə/
capital /ˈkæpɪtəl/
cliff /klɪf/
coast /kəʊst/
desert /ˈdezət/
farmland /ˈfɑːmlænd/
forest /ˈfɒrɪst/
island /ˈaɪlənd/
mountain /ˈmaʊntɪn/
ocean /ˈəʊʃən/
population /ˌpɒpjəˈleɪʃən/
port /pɔːt/
region /ˈriːdʒən/
river /ˈrɪvə/
scenery /ˈsiːnəri/
sea /siː/
soil /sɔɪl/
stream /striːm/
valley /ˈvæli/
waterfall /ˈwɔːtəfɔːl/

Adjectives
beautiful /ˈbjuːtɪfəl/
fast-flowing /ˌfɑːst ˈfləʊɪŋ/
rocky /ˈrɒki/
sandy /ˈsændi/
steep-sided /stiːp ˈsaɪdɪd/
thick /θɪk/

UNIT 2

APPEARANCES

Nouns
adult /ˈædʌlt/
baby /ˈbeɪbi/
beard /bɪəd/
child /tʃaɪld/
childhood /ˈtʃaɪldhʊd/
moustache /məˈstɑːʃ/
pensioner /ˈpenʃənə/
teenager /ˈtiːnˌeɪdʒə/
youth /juːθ/

Adjectives
attractive /əˈtræktɪv/
bald /bɔːld/
beautiful /ˈbjuːtɪfəl/
blonde /blɒnd/
bright /braɪt/
curly /ˈkɜːli/
dark /dɑːk/
elderly /ˈeldəli/
fair /feə/
fat /fæt/
good-looking /ˌgʊdˈlʊkɪŋ/
handsome /ˈhænsəm/
light /laɪt/
long /lɒŋ/
middle-aged /ˌmɪdəlˈeɪdʒd/
old /əʊld/
pale /peɪl/
pretty /ˈprɪti/
short /ʃɔːt/
slim /slɪm/
smart /smɑːt/
straight /streɪt/
tall /tɔːl/
teenage /ˈtiːneɪdʒ/
thin /θɪn/
ugly /ˈʌgli/
young /jʌŋ/

CLOTHES

Nouns
belt /belt/
blouse /blaʊz/
boots /buːts/
button /ˈbʌtən/
cap /kæp/

coat /kəʊt/
collar /ˈkɒlə/
dress /dres/
earrings /ˈɪərɪŋz/
glasses /ˈglɑːsɪz/
gloves /glʌvz/
handbag /ˈhænbæg/
handkerchief /ˈhæŋkətʃiːf/
hat /hæt/
jacket /ˈdʒækɪt/
jeans /dʒiːnz/
jewellery /ˈdʒuːəlri/
jumper /ˈdʒʌmpə/
lipstick /ˈlɪpstɪk/
perfume /ˈpɜːfjuːm/
pocket /ˈpɒkɪt/
pullover /ˈpʊləʊvə/
pyjamas /pɪˈdʒɑːməz/
raincoat /ˈreɪnkəʊt/
ring /rɪŋ/
shirt /ʃɜːt/
shoes /ʃuːz/
shorts /ʃɔːts/
skirt /skɜːt/
sleeves /sliːvz/
spots /spɒts/
suit /suːt/
sweater /ˈswetə/
sweatshirt /ˈswetʃɜːt/
swimming costume /ˈswɪmɪŋ ˈkɒstjuːm/
T-shirt /ˈtiːʃɜːt/
tie /taɪ/
tracksuit /ˈtræksuːt/
trainers /ˈtreɪnəz/
trousers /ˈtraʊzəz/
umbrella /ʌmˈbrelə/
uniform /ˈjuːnɪfɔːm/
watch /wɒtʃ/

Adjectives
comfortable /ˈkʌmftəbl/
cotton /ˈkɒtən/
fashionable /ˈfæʃənəbl/
gold /gəʊld/
knitted /ˈnɪtɪd/
leather /ˈleðə/
loose /luːs/
old-fashioned /ˌəʊldˈfæʃənd/
plastic /ˈplæstɪk/
silk /sɪlk/

silver /'sɪlvə/
stylish /'staɪlɪʃ/
tight /taɪt/
valuable /'væljʊbl/
woollen /'wʊlən/

Verbs/Verb phrases
fit /fɪt/
fold /fəʊld/
go with
match /mætʃ/
put on
take off
try on
wear out

UNIT 3

BEST FRIENDS

Nouns
promise /'prɒmɪs/
secret /'siːkrət/

Verbs/Verb phrases
accept /ək'sept/
complain /kəm'pleɪn/
fall out with
get on with
help /help/
laugh /lɑːf/
lie /laɪ/
make up (again)
promise /'prɒmɪs/
remember /rɪ'membə/
respect /rɪ'spekt/
share /ʃeə/
trust /trʌst/

PERSONALITIES AND SOCIAL INTERACTION

Adjectives
amazed /ə'meɪzd/
amazing /ə'meɪzɪŋ/
annoyed /ə'nɔɪd/
annoying /ə'nɔɪɪŋ/
anxious /'æŋkʃəs/
calm /kɑːm/
cheerful /'tʃɪəfəl/
confident /'kɒnfɪdənt/
cross /krɒs/
disappointed /dɪsəpɔɪntɪd/
disappointing /dɪsəpɔɪntɪŋ/
dull /dʌl/
embarrassed /ɪmbærəst/
embarrassing /ɪmbærəsɪŋ/
excited /ɪk'saɪtɪd/
exciting /ɪk'saɪtɪŋ/
fashionable /'fæʃənəbl/

funny /'fʌni/
generous /'dʒenərəs/
gentle /'dʒentl/
happy /'hæpi/
honest /'ɒnɪst/
interested /ɪntrəstɪd/
interesting /ɪntrəstɪŋ/
lazy /'leɪzi/
miserable /'mɪzrəbl/
nervous /'nɜːvəs/
reliable /rɪ'laɪəbl/
relaxed /rɪlækst/
relaxing /rɪlæksɪŋ/
sensible /'sensɪbl/
serious /'sɪəriəs/
shy /ʃaɪ/
silly /'sɪli/
stupid /'stjuːpɪd/
tired /taɪəd/
tiring /'taɪərɪŋ/
upset /ʌp'set/

UNIT 4

RELATIVES AND RELATIONSHIPS

Nouns
aunt /ɑːnt/
brother /'brʌðə/
cousin /'kʌzən/
daughter /'dɔːtə/
father /'fɑːðə/
father in law /'fɑːðər ɪn lɔː/
granddaughter /'græn,dɔːtə/
grandfather /'græn,fɑːðə/
grandmother /'græn,mʌðə/
grandson /'grænsʌn/
husband /'hʌzbənd/
mother /'mʌðə/
mother in law /'mʌðər ɪn lɔː/
nephew /'nefjuː/
niece /niːs/
parents /'peərənts/
sister /'sɪstə/
son /sʌn/
uncle /'ʌŋkl/
wife /waɪf/

Verb phrases
bring up
find out
get on (with)
get up
give up
go out (with)
grow up
keep in
keep on

look after
look forward to
move in (with)
run out of

DAILY LIFE

Verb phrases
brush your hair/teeth
catch the bus/the train
eat breakfast/lunch/dinner
get dressed/undressed/ready
go swimming/jogging
go to school/college/work
have a bath/shower/wash
leave home/work
meet friends

SPECIAL OCCASIONS

Nouns
anniversary /,ænɪ'vɜːsəri/
bride /braɪd/
cake /keɪk/
guest /gest/
invitation /,ɪnvɪ'teɪʃən/
party /'pɑːti/
reception /rɪ'sepʃən/
ring /rɪŋ/
speech /spiːtʃ/
wedding /'wedɪŋ/

UNIT 5

DESCRIBING YOUR HOME

Nouns
air-conditioning /eə kən'dɪʃənɪŋ/
balcony /'bælkəni/
basement /'beɪsmənt/
bathroom /'bɑːθrʊm/
bedroom /'bedrʊm/
CD player /siːdiː 'pleɪə/
cellar /'selə/
central heating
chimney /'tʃɪmni/
clothes line /kləʊðz laɪn/
computer /kəm'pjuːtə/
cooker /'kʊkə/
corkscrew /'kɔːkskruː/
desk /desk/
dining room /daɪnɪŋ ruːm/
dishwasher /'dɪʃ,wɒʃə/
DVD player /diːviːdiː 'pleɪə/
entrance /'entrəns/
fence /fens/
freezer /'friːzə/

frying pan /fraɪŋ pæn/
garage /'gærɑːʒ/
garden /'gɑːdən/
gate /geɪt/
hall /hɔːl/
hedge /hedʒ/
hi-fi /'haɪfaɪ/
iron /aɪən/
jug /dʒʌg/
kitchen /'kɪtʃɪn/
lawn /lɔːn/
living room /lɪvɪŋ ruːm/
lounge /laʊndʒ/
microwave /'maɪkrəweɪv/
path /pɑːθ/
plants /plɑːnts/
roof /ruːf/
rubbish bin /'rʌbɪʃ bɪn/
seat /siːt/
shaver /'ʃeɪvə/
sitting room /sɪtɪŋ ruːm/
sofa /'səʊfə/
space /speɪs/
steps /steps/
table /'teɪbl/
toilet /'tɔɪlət/
tools /tuːlz/
toothpaste /'tuːθpeɪst/
TV /,tiː'viː/
video recorder /vɪdiəʊ rɪkɔːdə/
walls /wɔːlz/
washing machine /wɒʃɪŋ mə'ʃiːn/
windows /'wɪndəʊz/

Adjectives
comfortable /'kʌmftəbl/
convenient /kən'viːniənt/
lively /'laɪvli/
neat /niːt/
peaceful /'piːsfəl/
tidy /'taɪdi/

KITCHEN AND LIVING ROOM

Nouns
antiques /æn'tiːks/
armchair /'ɑːmtʃeə/
carpet /'kɑːpɪt/
cleaning products /'kliːnɪŋ 'prɒdʌktz/
cupboard /'kʌbəd/
curtains /'kɜːtənz/
cushions /'kʊʃənz/
drawer /drɔː/
edge /edʒ/
electrical items /ɪ'lektrɪkl aɪtəms/
fan /fæn/

floor /flɔː/
handle /'hændl/
kettle /'ketl/
knives /naɪvz/
lamp /læmp/
plug /plʌg/
switch /swɪtʃ/
television /'telɪvɪʒən/
toys /tɔɪz/
vase /vɑːz/

BEDROOM AND BATHROOM

Nouns

alarm clock /əl'ɑːm klɒk/
basin /'beɪsən/
blind /blaɪnd/
chest of drawers
  /tʃest əv 'drɔːz/
duvet /'duːveɪ/
mirror /'mɪrə/
pillow /'pɪləʊ/
radio /'reɪdiəʊ/
rubbish bin /'rʌbɪʃ bɪn/
sheet /ʃiːt/
shelf /ʃelf/
tap /tæp/
towel /taʊəl/

UNIT 6

THE ENVIRONMENT

Nouns

bottle bank /'bɒtl bæŋk/
cans /kænz/
cardboard /'kɑːdbɔːd/
climate change /klaɪmət
  tʃeɪndʒ/
coal /kəʊl/
countryside /'kʌntrɪsaɪd/
electricity /ɪlek'trɪsəti/
environment /ɪn'vaɪrəmənt/
floods /flʌdz/
fuel /'fjuːəl/
glass /glɑːs/
global warming /glaʊbl wɔːmɪŋ/
litter /'lɪtə/
metal /'metəl/
nature /'neɪtʃə/
packaging /'pækɪdʒɪŋ/
paper /'peɪpə/
petrol /'petrəl/
plants /plɑːnts/
plastic /'plæstɪk/
pollution /pə'luːʃən/
public transport /pʌblɪk
  træn'spɔːt/

rainforests /'reɪn,fɒrɪsts/
rubbish /'rʌbɪʃ/
storms /stɔːmz/
tins /tɪnz/
traffic jams /'træfɪk dʒæmz/
transport /'trænspɔːt/
waste /weɪst/
wildlife /'waɪldlaɪf/

OPINION AND ATTITUDE

Verbs

advise /əd'vaɪz/
agree /ə'griː/
compare /kəm'peə/
complain /kəm'pleɪn/
decide /dɪ'saɪd/
describe /dɪ'skraɪb/
disagree /,dɪsə'griː/
discuss /dɪ'skʌs/
encourage /ɪn'kʌrɪdʒ/
explain /ɪk'spleɪn/
persuade /pə'sweɪd/
promise /'prɒmɪs/
recommend /,rekə'mend/
remind /rɪ'maɪnd/
review /rɪ'vjuː/
suggest /sə'dʒest/
warn /wɔːn/

FEELINGS

Adjectives

afraid /ə'freɪd/
amazed /ə'meɪzd/
angry /'æŋgri/
annoyed /ə'nɔɪd/
anxious /'æŋkʃəs/
ashamed /ə'ʃeɪmd/
calm /kɑːm/
delighted /dɪ'laɪtɪd/
depressed /dɪ'prest/
disappointed /,dɪsə'pɔɪntɪd/
embarrassed /ɪm'bærəst/
frightened /'fraɪtənd/
miserable /'mɪzrəbl/
pleased /pliːzd/
relaxed /rɪ'lækst/
satisfied /'sætɪsfaɪd/
surprised /sə'praɪzd/
upset /'ʌpset/
worried /'wʌrid/

Verbs/Verb phrases

be fond of
be keen on
dislike /dɪ'slaɪk/
hate /heɪt/
look forward to

love /lʌv/
mind /maɪnd/

UNIT 7

SHOPPING

Nouns

bill /bɪl/
cash /kæʃ/
charge /tʃɑːdʒ/
cheque /tʃek/
credit card /'kredɪt kɑːd/
customer /'kʌstəmə/
deposit /dɪ'pɒzɪt/
discount /'dɪskaʊnt/
receipt /rɪ'siːt/
refund /'riːfʌnd/

ON THE HIGH STREET

Nouns

assistant /ə'sɪstənt/
checkout /'tʃekaʊt/
chemist /'kemɪst/
department store /dɪ'pɑːtmənt
  stɔː/
display /dɪ'spleɪ/
dry cleaner /draɪ 'kliːnə/
escalator /'eskəleɪtə/
hairdresser /'heə,dresə/
jeweller /'dʒuːələ/
lift /lɪft/
manager /'mænɪdʒə/
pharmacy /'fɑːməsi/
photographer /fə'tɒgrəfə/
post office /pəʊst 'ɒfɪs/
salesman /'seɪlzmən/
take-away /teɪk ə'weɪ/
travel agent /trævl eɪdʒənt/

UNIT 8

EATING OUT

Nouns

diet /daɪət/
dessert /dɪ'zɜːt/
drinks /drɪŋks/
main course /meɪn kɔːs/
menu /'menjuː/
snack /snæk/
starter /'stɑːtə/
tip /tɪp/
waiter /'weɪtə/

FOOD AND DRINK

Nouns

apple /'æpl/
banana /bə'nɑːnə/
bean /biːn/
biscuit /'bɪskɪt/
bread /bred/
burger /'bɜːgə/
butter /'bʌtə/
cabbage /'kæbɪdʒ/
cake /keɪk/
candy /'kændi/
carrot /'kærət/
cauliflower /'kɒlɪ,flaʊə/
celery /'seləri/
cereal /'sɪəriəl/
chicken /'tʃɪkɪn/
chips /tʃɪps/
chocolate /'tʃɒkələt/
coconut /'kəʊkənʌt/
cod /kɒd/
coffee /'kɒfi/
coke /kəʊk/
cookie /'kʊki/
cream /kriːm/
cucumber /'kjuːkʌmbə/
duck /dʌk/
egg /eg/
flour /flaʊə/
grape /greɪp/
ham /hæm/
honey /'hʌni/
ice cream /,aɪs'kriːm/
jam /dʒæm/
juice /dʒuːs/
lamb /læm/
lemon /'lemən/
lemonade /,lemə'neɪd/
lettuce /'letɪs/
melon /'melən/
milk /mɪlk/
mineral water /mɪnərəl wɔːtə/
mushroom /'mʌʃrʊm/
omelette /'ɒmlət/
pastry /'peɪstri/
pear /peə/
pepper /'pepə/
pie /paɪ/
pizza /'piːtsə/
plaice /pleɪs/
potato /pə'teɪtəʊ/
raisin /'reɪzən/
roll /rəʊl/
salad /'sæləd/
sausage /'sɒsɪdʒ/
soft drink /sɒft drɪŋk/
spinach /'spɪnɪtʃ/
steak /steɪk/

strawberry /'strɔːbəri/
sugar /'ʃʊgə/
tart /tɑːt/
tea /tiː/
toast /təʊst/
tomato /tə'mɑːtəʊ/
turkey /'tɜːki/
vanilla /və'nɪlə/

CONTAINERS AND AMOUNTS

Nouns
bowl /bəʊl/
can /kæn/
cup /kʌp/
dish /dɪʃ/
jug /dʒʌg/
kettle /'ketl/
loaf /ləʊf/
mug /mʌg/
packet /'pækɪt/
pan /pæn/
piece /piːs/
plate /pleɪt/
saucer /'sɔːsə/
slice /slaɪs/
spoonful /'spuːnfʊl/

TASTE

Adjectives
bitter /'bɪtə/
raw /rɔː/
sour /saʊə/
sweet /swiːt/

COOKING

Nouns
ingredient /ɪn'griːdiənt/
instruction /ɪn'strʌkʃən/
recipe /'resɪpi/

Verbs
add /æd/
bake /beɪk/
barbecue /'bɑːbɪkjuː/
beat /biːt/
boil /bɔɪl/
burn /bɜːn/
cook /kʊk/
cut /kʌt/
fry /fraɪ/
grill /grɪl/
mix /mɪks/
pour /pɔː/
roast /rəʊst/
stir /stɜː/
taste /teɪst/

UNIT 9

PUBLIC TRANSPORT

Nouns
airline /'eəlaɪn/
airport /'eəpɔːt/
arrivals /ə'raɪvəlz/
baggage collection /bægɪdʒ kəlekʃən/
boarding pass /bɔːdɪŋ pɑːs/
check-in /'tʃekɪn/
customs /'kʌstəmz/
delay /dɪ'leɪ/
departure lounge /dɪpaːtʃə laʊndʒ/
destination /,destɪ'neɪʃən/
driver /'draɪvə/
duty-free /,djuːti'friː/
fare /feə/
flight /flaɪt/
flight attendant /flaɪt ə'tendənt/
gate /geɪt/
immigration /,ɪmɪ'greɪʃən/
lost property /lɒst prɒpəti/
luggage /'lʌgɪdʒ/
passenger /'pæsəndʒə/
pilot /'paɪlət/
platform /'plætfɔːm/
refund /'riːfʌnd/
safety demonstration /seɪfti demən'streɪʃən/
security /sɪ'kjʊərəti/
station /'steɪʃən/
terminal /'tɜːmɪnəl/
timetable /'taɪm,teɪbl/
waiting room /weɪtɪŋ ruːm/

Adjectives
by air
by land
by rail
by road
by sea
cheap /tʃiːp/
comfortable /'kʌmftəbl/
convenient /kən'viːniənt/
crowded /'kraʊdɪd/
dangerous /'deɪndʒərəs/
empty /'empti/
expensive /ɪk'spensɪv/
inconvenient /,ɪnkən'viːniənt/
noisy /'nɔɪzi/
quiet /kwaɪət/
reliable /rɪ'laɪəbl/
safe /seɪf/
uncomfortable /ʌn'kʌmftəbl/
unreliable /,ʌnrɪ'laɪəbl/

Verbs/Verb phrases
board /bɔːd/
check in
fasten your seatbelt
land /lænd/
take off

HOLIDAYS

Nouns
adventure /əd'ventʃə/
backpack /'bækpæk/
backpacker /'bækpækə/
bed and breakfast /bed ən 'brekfəst/
break /breɪk/
brochure /'brəʊʃə/
camper /'kæmpə/
campsite /'kæmpsaɪt/
climber /'klaɪmə/
culture /'kʌltʃə/
cyclist /'saɪklɪst/
driver /'draɪvə/
facilities /fə'sɪlətiz/
guest /gest/
guesthouse /'gesthaʊs/
guide book /gaɪd bʊk/
hitchhiker /'hɪtʃhaɪkə/
hostel /'hɒstəl/
hotel /həʊtel/
inn /ɪn/
interpreter /ɪn'tɜːprɪtə/
receptionist /rɪ'sepʃənɪst/
room service /ruːm 'sɜːvɪs/
route /ruːt/
single room /sɪŋl ruːm/
souvenir shop /suːvən'ɪə ʃɒp/
taxi rank /'tæksi ræŋk/
tent /tent/
tourist /'tʊərɪst/
track /træk/
translator /trænz'leɪtə/
traveller /'trævələ/
view /vjuː/

Adjectives
distant /'dɪstənt/
leisure /'leʒə/
luxury /'lʌkʃəri/
overnight /,əʊvə'naɪt/

Verbs/Verb phrases
book /bʊk/
camp /kæmp/
check out
cycle /'saɪkl/
explore /ɪk'splɔː/
pack /pæk/
relax /rɪ'læks/
reserve /rɪ'zɜːv/
sightsee /'saɪtsiː/
ski /skiː/
tour /tʊə/

UNIT 10

HOBBIES

Nouns
cooking /'kʊkɪŋ/
cycling /'saɪklɪŋ/
gymnastics /dʒɪm'næstɪks/
horse-riding /hɔːs 'raɪdɪŋ/
keep fit /kiːp fɪt/
knitting /'nɪtɪŋ/
painting /'peɪntɪŋ/
photography /fə'tɒgrəfi/
sewing /'səʊɪŋ/
skiing /'skiːɪŋ/

Verbs
arrange /ə'reɪndʒ/
build /bɪld/
buy /baɪ/
collect /'kɒlekt/
exchange /ɪks'tʃeɪndʒ/
increase /'ɪnkriːs/
perform /pə'fɔːm/
practice /'præktɪs/
stick /stɪk/

OUTDOOR AND INDOOR LEISURE ACTIVITIES

Nouns
boots /buːts/
camping /'kæmpɪŋ/
campsite /'kæmpsaɪt/
climbing /'klaɪmɪŋ/
clothing /'kləʊðɪŋ/
club /klʌb/
dancing /'dɑːnsɪŋ/
equipment /ɪ'kwɪpmənt/
fee /fiː/
helmet /'helmət/
life jacket /laɪf dʒækɪt/
member /'membə/
membership (card) /'membəʃɪp/
sailing /'seɪlɪŋ/
society /sə'saɪəti/
tent /tent/

ARRANGING A PARTY

Nouns
band /bænd/
barbecue /'bɑːbɪkjuː/
disc jockey /dɪsk 'dʒɒki/
disco /'dɪskəʊ/
invitations /,ɪnvɪ'teɪʃənz/
neighbours /'neɪbəz/
venue /'venjuː/

UNIT 11

SUBJECTS

Nouns

art /ɑːt/
biology /baɪˈɒlədʒi/
chemistry /ˈkemɪstri/
drama /ˈdrɑːmə/
economics /ˌiːkəˈnɒmɪks/
English /ˈɪŋglɪʃ/
French /frenʃ/
geography /dʒiˈɒgrəfi/
history /ˈhɪstəri/
information technology
　　/ɪnfəmeɪʃən teknɒlədʒi/
languages /ˈlæŋgwɪdʒɪz/
literature /ˈlɪtrətʃə/
mathematics /mæθəmˈætɪks/
music /ˈmjuːzɪk/
photography /fəˈtɒgrəfi/
physics /ˈfɪzɪks/
science /saɪəns/
Spanish /ˈspænɪʃ/
sport /spɔːt/

Adjectives

boring /ˈbɔːrɪŋ/
difficult /ˈdɪfɪkəlt/
dull /dʌl/
easy /ˈiːzi/
enjoyable /ɪnˈdʒɔɪəbl/
hard /hɑːd/
important /ɪmˈpɔːtənt/
interesting /ˈɪntrəstɪŋ/
pointless /ˈpɔɪntləs/
useful /ˈjuːsfəl/
useless /ˈjuːsləs/

TEACHING AND STUDYING

Nouns

bell /bel/
board /bɔːd/
break /breɪk/
certificate /səˈtɪfɪkət/
college /ˈkɒlɪdʒ/
composition /ˌkɒmpəˈzɪʃən/
curriculum /kəˈrɪkjələm/
degree /dɪˈgriː/
equipment /ɪˈkwɪpmənt/
essay /ˈeseɪ/
failure /ˈfeɪljə/
grade /greɪd/
instructor /ɪnˈstrʌktə/
laboratory /ləˈbɒrətəri/
lecturer /ˈlektʃərə/
methods /ˈmeθədz/
primary school /praɪˈməri skuːl/

professor /prəˈfesə/
pupil /ˈpjuːpəl/
qualification /ˌkwɒlɪfɪˈkeɪʃən/
report /rɪˈpɔːt/
result /rɪˈzʌlt/
rubber /ˈrʌbə/
ruler /ˈruːlə/
secondary school /sekəndri
　　skuːl/
teacher /ˈtiːtʃə/
text book /tekst bʊk/
trainer /ˈtreɪnə/
university /ˌjuːnɪˈvɜːsəti/
welfare /ˈwelfeə/

Adjectives

absent /ˈæbsənt/
clever /ˈklevə/
fair /feə/
funny /ˈfʌni/
intelligent /ɪnˈtelɪdʒənt/
kind /kaɪnd/
patient /ˈpeɪʃənt/
punctual /ˈpʌŋktʃuəl/
reasonable /ˈriːzənəbl/
serious /ˈsɪəriəs/
strict /strɪkt/

Verbs/Verb phrases

fail an exam
hand in homework
learn /lɜːn/
make progress
mark homework
pass an exam
pay attention
revise /rɪˈvaɪz/
study /ˈstʌdi/
take an exam

LEARNING A LANGUAGE

Nouns

grammar /ˈgræmə/
pronunciation
　　/prəˌnʌnsiˈeɪʃən/
reading /ˈriːdɪŋ/
speaking /ˈspiːkɪŋ/
spelling /ˈspelɪŋ/
vocabulary /vəˈkæbjələri/
writing /ˈraɪtɪŋ/

Verbs

interpret /ɪnˈtɜːprɪt/
say /seɪ/
translate /trænzˈleɪt/

UNIT 12

ACHES AND PAINS

Nouns

ankle /ˈæŋkl/
arm /ɑːm/
back /bæk/
bone /bəʊn/
chin /tʃɪn/
ear /ɪə/
eye /aɪ/
finger /ˈfɪŋgə/
foot /fʊt/
hair /heə/
head /hed/
knee /niː/
leg /leg/
mouth /maʊθ/
neck /nek/
shoulder /ˈʃəʊldə/
skin /skɪn/
throat /θrəʊt/
thumb /θʌm/
toes /təʊz/
backache /ˈbækeɪk/
cold /kəʊld/
cough /kɒf/
earache /ˈɪəreɪk/
flu /fluː/
headache /ˈhedeɪk/
stomach ache /ˈstʌmək eɪk/
temperature /ˈtemprətʃə/
toothache /ˈtuːθeɪk/

TREATMENT

Nouns

accident /ˈæksɪdənt/
ambulance /ˈæmbjələns/
appointment /əˈpɔɪntmənt/
bandage /ˈbændɪdʒ/
chemist /ˈkemɪst/
dentist /ˈdentɪst/
doctor /ˈdɒktə/
dressing /ˈdresɪŋ/
glasses /ˈglɑːsɪz/
hospital /ˈhɒspɪtəl/
medicine /ˈmedɪsən/
nurse /nɜːs/
patient /ˈpeɪʃənt/
plaster /ˈplɑːstə/
prescription /prɪˈskrɪpʃən/

Verbs/Verb phrases

ache /eɪk/
be injured
break (a bone) /breɪk/
burn (yourself) /bɜːn/
catch (an illness) /kætʃ/
cut /kʌt/

feel (well/ill/better/sick) /fiːl/
get (better/worse) /get/
hurt /hɜːt/
put on weight
taste /teɪst/

HEALTHY LIVING

Nouns

exercise /ˈeksəsaɪz/
fat /fæt/
gym /dʒɪm/
leisure /ˈleʒə/
lifestyle /ˈlaɪfstaɪl/
liquid /ˈlɪkwɪd/
park /pɑːk/

Adjectives

active /ˈæktɪv/
filling /ˈfɪlɪŋ/
fit /fɪt/
healthy /ˈhelθi/
hungry /ˈhʌŋgri/
inactive /ɪnˈæktɪv/
sensible /ˈsensɪbl/
thirsty /ˈθɜːsti/

Verbs/Verb phrases

aim for
be active
cycle /ˈsaɪkl/
feel/get/keep fit
get off /
use /juːs/
walk /wɔːk/

Adverbs

properly /ˈprɒpəli/
regularly /ˈregjələli/

UNIT 13

SPORTS

Nouns

ball /bɔːl/
basket /ˈbɑːskɪt/
basketball /ˈbɑːskɪtbɔːl/
bat /bæt/
boxing /ˈbɒksɪŋ/
cycling /ˈsaɪklɪŋ/
diving /ˈdaɪvɪŋ/
fishing /ˈfɪʃɪŋ/
fishing rod /ˈfɪʃɪŋ rɒd/
football /ˈfʊtbɔːl/
gloves /glʌvz/
goal /gəʊl/
golf /gɒlf/
gymnastics /dʒɪmˈnæstɪks/
helmet /ˈhelmət/
hockey /ˈhɒki/

horse-riding /hɔːs 'raɪdɪŋ/
jogging /'dʒɒgɪŋ/
marathon /'mærəθən/
match /mætʃ/
net /net/
race-course /reɪs kɔːs/
racket /'rækɪt/
result /rɪ'zʌlt/
running /'rʌnɪŋ/
sailing /'seɪlɪŋ/
score /skɔː/
skiing /'skiːɪŋ/
skis /skiːz/
squash /skwɒʃ/
stadium /'steɪdiəm/
stick /stɪk/
swimming /'swɪmɪŋ/
table tennis /'teɪbl 'tenɪs/
tennis /'tenɪs/
track /træk/
volleyball /'vɒlibɔːl/
weightlifting /'weɪt,lɪftɪŋ/
weights /weɪts/

PEOPLE

Nouns

champion /'tʃæmpiən/
coach /kəʊtʃ/
partner /'pɑːtnə/
player /'pleɪə/
reserve /rɪ'zɜːv/
team /tiːm/
team-mate /tiːm meɪt/
trainer /'treɪnə/
winner /'wɪnə/

Verbs/Verb phrases

dive /daɪv/
join in
kick /kɪk/
play /pleɪ/
practise /'præktɪs/
score /skɔː/
swim /swɪm/
take part

FITNESS

Nouns

benefit /'benɪfɪt/
changing room /tʃeɪndʒɪŋ ruːm/
club /klʌb/
exercise bike /'eksəsaɪz baɪk/
gym /dʒɪm/
locker /'lɒkə/
sauna /'sɔːnə/
steam room /stiːm ruːm/
step machine /step mə'ʃiːn/
track suit /træk suːt/

Adjectives

strong /strɒŋ/
healthy /helθi/
confident /kɒnfɪdənt/

■ UNIT 14

ANIMALS

Nouns

animals /'ænɪməlz/
bat /bæt/
bear /beə/
bee /biː/
birds /bɜːdz/
bull /bʊl/
camel /'kæməl/
cat /kæt/
chicken /'tʃɪkɪn/
cow /kaʊ/
dog /dɒg/
dolphin /'dɒlfɪn/
duck /dʌk/
elephant /'elɪfənt/
farm animals /fɑːm 'ænɪməlz/
fish /fɪʃ/
fur /fɜː/
giraffe /dʒɪ'rɑːf/
goat /gəʊt/
horse /hɔːs/
insects /'ɪnsekts/
kitten /'kɪtən/
lamb /læm/
lion /laɪən/
monkey /'mʌŋki/
mouse /maʊs/
parrot /'pærət/
pets /pets/
pig /pɪg/
rabbit /'ræbɪt/
sea creatures /siː 'kriːtʃəz/
sheep /ʃiːp/
snake /sneɪk/
sting /stɪŋ/
teeth /tiːθ/
tiger /'taɪgə/
turkey /'tɜːki/
whale /weɪl/
wild animals /waɪld 'ænɪməlz/
wings /wɪŋz/
zebra /'zebrə/

Adjectives

amusing /ə'mjuːzɪŋ/
beautiful /'bjuːtɪfəl/
dangerous /'deɪndʒərəs/
friendly /'frendli/
frightening /'fraɪtənɪŋ/
useful /'juːsfəl/

THE COUNTRYSIDE

Nouns

bark /bɑːk/
beach /biːtʃ/
branch /brɑːnʃ/
canal /kə'næl/
cave /keɪv/
cliff /klɪf/
coast /kəʊst/
collar /'kɒlə/
desert /'dezət/
dolphin /'dɒlfɪn/
ears /ɪəz/
earth /ɜːθ/
eggs /egz/
farm /fɑːm/
farmer /'fɑːmə/
field /'fiːld/
fish /fɪʃ/
flowers /flaʊəz/
forest /'fɒrɪst/
fur /fɜː/
garden /'gɑːdən/
grass /grɑːs/
harbour /'hɑːbə/
hill /hɪl/
holiday /'hɒlɪdeɪ/
insect /'ɪnsekt/
island /'aɪlənd/
lake /leɪk/
lambs /læmz/
leaf /liːf/
moon /muːn/
ocean /'əʊʃən/
path /pɑːθ/
pet /pet/
planet /'plænɪt/
plant /plɑːnt/
river /'rɪvə/
rock /rɒk/
rose /rəʊz/
sand /sænd/
sea /siː/
seaside /'siːsaɪd/
sky /skaɪ/
snow /snəʊ/
soil /sɔɪl/
space /speɪs/
star /stɑː/
stream /striːm/
sun /sʌn/
universe /'juːnɪvɜːs/
valley /'væli/
waves /weɪvz/
wet /wet/
wood /wʊd/

Adjectives

deep /diːp/
high /haɪ/
soft /sɒft/

Verbs

climb /klaɪm/
flow /fləʊ/

■ UNIT 15

THE WEATHER

Nouns

cold /kəʊld/
degree centigrade /dɪ'griː 'sentɪgreɪd/
fog /fɒg/
frost /frɒst/
gale /geɪl/
heat /hiːt/
ice /aɪs/
lightening /'laɪtənɪŋ/
rain /reɪn/
shower /ʃaʊə/
snow /snəʊ/
storm /stɔːm/
sun /sʌn/
sunshine /'sʌnʃaɪn/
temperature /'temprətʃə/
thermometer /θə'mɒmɪtə/
thunder /'θʌndə/

Adjectives

cloudy /'klaʊdi/
cold /kəʊld/
foggy /'fɒgi/
frosty /'frɒsti/
hot /hɒt/
icy /'aɪsi/
rainy /'reɪniŋ/
showery /'ʃaʊəri/
snowy /'snəʊi/
stormy /'stɔːmi/
sunny /'sʌni/
windy /'wɪndi/

Verbs

burn /bɜːn/
rain /reɪn/
slip /slɪp/

FORECASTING THE WEATHER

Adjectives

bright /braɪt/
clean /kliːn/
clear /klɪə/
cool /kuːl/

dry /draɪ/
heavy /'hevi/
high /haɪ/
light /laɪt/
low /ləʊ/
mild /maɪld/
pleasant /'plezənt/
strong /strɒŋ/
warm /wɔːm/
weak /wiːk/
wet /wet/

CLIMATES AND SEASONS

Nouns
east /iːst/
north /nɔːθ/
northeast /ˌnɔːθ'iːst/
northwest /ˌnɔːθ'west/
south /saʊθ/
southeast /ˌsaʊθ'iːst/
southwest /ˌsaʊθ'west/
west /west/

autumn /'ɔːtəm/
fall (US English) /fɔːl/
spring /sprɪŋ/
summer /'sʌmə/
winter /'wɪntə/

January /'dʒænjuəri/
February /'februəri/
March /mɑːtʃ/
April /'eɪprəl/
May /meɪ/
June /dʒuːn/
July /dʒʊ'laɪ/
August /'ɔːgəst/
September /sep'tembə/
October /ɒk'təʊbə/
November /nəʊ'vembə/
December /dɪ'sembə/

Adjectives
average /'ævərɪdʒ/
typical /'tɪpɪkəl/

UNIT 16

TELEVISION

Nouns
cartoon /kɑː'tuːn/
channel /'tʃænəl/
character /'kærəktə/
current affairs /kʌrənt ə'feaz/
discussion /dɪ'skʌʃən/
documentary /ˌdɒkjʊ'mentəri/
drama /'drɑːmə/
hero /'hɪərəʊ/
natural history /nætʃərəl
    'hɪstəri/

play /pleɪ/
presenter /prɪ'zentə/
programmes /'prəʊgræmz/
quiz /kwɪz/
series /'sɪəriːz/
sitcom /'sɪtkɒm/
soap /səʊp/
thriller /'θrɪlə/
weather forecast /'weðə
    'fɔːkɑːst/

READING BOOKS

adventure /əd'ventʃə/
biography /baɪ'ɒgrəfi/
fiction /'fɪkʃən/
historical/fantasy/romantic/
    mystery novel
horror /'hɒrə/
love /lʌv/
non-fiction /nɒn 'fɪkʃən/
science fiction /saɪəns 'fɪkʃən/
thriller /'θrɪlə/

NEWSPAPERS AND MAGAZINES

Nouns
article /'ɑːtɪkəl/
headlines /'hedlaɪnz/
journalist /'dʒɜːnəlɪst/
photograph /'fəʊtəgrɑːf/
report /rɪ'pɔːt/
reporter /rɪ'pɔːtə/
review /rɪ'vjuː/

Adjectives
daily /'deɪli/
weekly /'wiːkli/
fortnightly /'fɔːtnaɪtli/
monthly /'mʌnθli/
annually /'ænjuəli/

UNIT 17

TOWNS AND CITIES

Nouns
atmosphere /'ætməsfɪə/
bar /bɑː/
bookshop /'bʊkʃɒp/
bus station /bʌs 'steɪʃən/
castle /'kɑːsəl/
chemist /'kemɪst/
church /tʃɜːtʃ/
clinic /'klɪnɪk/
coffee shop /'kɒfi ʃɒp/
dentist /'dentɪst/
disco /'dɪskəʊ/
drycleaner /draɪ'kliːnə/

gallery /'gæləri/
guesthouse /'gesthaʊs/
hairdresser /'heəˌdresə/
hotel /həʊ'tel/
mosque /mɒsk/
museum /mjuː'ziːəm/
newsagent /'njuːzˌeɪdʒənt/
noise /nɔɪz/
office block /'ɒfɪs blɒk/
palace /'pælɪs/
park /pɑːk/
peace and quiet /piːs ən
    kwaɪət/
pedestrian crossing
    /pɪ'destriən 'krɒsɪŋ/
pollution /pə'luːʃən/
public transport /'pʌblɪk
    'trænspɔːt/
railway station /'reɪlweɪ
    'steɪʃən/
roundabout /'raʊndəˌbaʊt/
scenery /'siːnəri/
shopping centre /'ʃɒpɪŋ 'sentə/
signpost /'saɪnpəʊst/
stadium /'steɪdiəm/
supermarket /'suːpəˌmɑːkɪt/
swimming pool /'swɪmɪŋ puːl/
theatre /'θɪətə/
traffic jams /'træfɪk dʒæmz/
traffic lights /'træfɪk laɪts/
turning /'tɜːnɪŋ/
village /'vɪlɪdʒ/
zoo /zuː/

Adjectives
boring /'bɔːrɪŋ/
beautiful /'bjuːtɪfəl/
busy /'bɪzi/
clean /kliːn/
convenient /kən'viːniənt/
crowded /'kraʊdɪd/
dangerous /'deɪndʒərəs/
dirty /'dɜːti/
exciting /ɪk'saɪtɪŋ/
lively /'laɪvli/
quiet /kwaɪət/
safe /seɪf/

PLACES AND BUILDINGS

Nouns
factory /'fæktəri/
office /'ɒfɪs/
car park /kɑː pɑːk/
cathedral /kə'θiːdrəl/
corner /'kɔːnə/
cottage /'kɒtɪdʒ/
field /'fiːld/

crossroads /'krɒsrəʊdz/
farm /fɑːm/
hospital /'hɒspɪtəl/

VEHICLES

Nouns
aeroplane /'eərəpleɪn/
bell /bel/
bicycle /'baɪsɪkl/
boot /buːt/
brake /breɪk/
bus /bʌs/
cab /kæb/
cabin /'kæbɪn/
car /kɑː/
coach /kəʊtʃ/
engine /'endʒɪn/
ferry /'feri/
handlebars /'hændəlbɑːz/
helicopter /'helɪkɒptə/
hovercraft /'hɒvəkrɑːft/
lorry /'lɒri/
motorbike /'məʊtəbaɪk/
seatbelt /siːtbelt/
scooter /'skuːtə/
ship /ʃɪp/
taxi /'tæksi/
train /treɪn/
tram /træm/
truck /trʌk/
tyres /'taɪəz/
underground train
    /ʌndə'graʊnd treɪn/
wheels /wiːlz/
wings /wɪŋz/

UNIT 18

THE ARTS

Nouns
ballet /'bæleɪ/
comedy /'kɒmədi/
concert /'kɒnsət/
dance /dɑːns/
drama /'drɑːmə/
exhibition /ˌeksɪ'bɪʃən/
film /fɪlm/
jazz /dʒæz/
musical /'mjuːzɪkəl/
novel /'nɒvəl/
poem /'pəʊɪm/
opera /'ɒpərə/
orchestra /'ɔːkɪstrə/
play /pleɪ/

THEATRE AND MUSIC

Nouns

actor /'æktə/
audience /'ɔːdiəns/
box office /bɒks 'ɒfɪs/
character /'kærəktə/
classical/pop/rock music
costume /'kɒstjuːm/
curtain /'kɜːtən/
drums /drʌmz/
flute /fluːt/
guitar /gɪ'tɑː/
hero /'hɪərəʊ/
interval /'ɪntəvəl/
instrument /'ɪnstrəmənt/
keyboard /'kiːbɔːd/
lighting /'laɪtɪŋ/
make-up /'meɪkʌp/
musician /mjuː'zɪʃən/
performance /pə'fɔːməns/
piano /pi'ænəʊ/
role /rəʊl/
scene /siːn/
scenery /'siːnəri/
sound /saʊnd/
stage /steɪdʒ/
star /stɑː/
ticket /'tɪkɪt/
trumpet /'trʌmpɪt/
violin /ˌvaɪə'lɪn/

Verbs

act /ækt/
clap /klæp/
direct /daɪ'rekt/
perform /pə'fɔːm/
play /pleɪ/
produce /prə'djuːs/
show /ʃəʊ/
star (in) /stɑː/

CINEMA

action /'ækʃən/
animation /ˌænɪ'meɪʃən/
cartoon /kɑː'tuːn/
comedy /'kɒmədi/
drama /'drɑːmə/
fantasy /'fæntəsi/
historical /hɪ'stɒrɪkəl/
horror /'hɒrə/
mystery /'mɪstəri/
romantic /rə'mæntɪk/
science fiction /saɪəns 'fɪkʃən/
thriller /'θrɪlə/

COMMUNICATING

Nouns

conversation /ˌkɒnvə'seɪʃən/
email /'iːmeɪl/
landline /'lændlaɪn/
letter /'letə/
mobile(phone) /'məʊbaɪl/
note /nəʊt/
telephone /'telɪfəʊn/
text message /tekst 'mesɪdʒ/

Verbs

call /kɔːl/
email /'iːmeɪl/
phone /fəʊn/
speak /spiːk/
text /tekst/
write /raɪt/

COMPUTERS

Nouns

application /ˌæplɪ'keɪʃən/
chatroom /'tʃætruːm/
disc /dɪsk/
games /geɪmz/
hard drive /hɑːd draɪv/
homework /'həʊmwɜːk/
internet /'ɪntənet/
keyboard /'kiːbɔːd/
laptop /'læptɒp/
memory /'meməri/
mouse /maʊs/
password /'pɑːswɜːd/
program/programme /
  prəʊgræm/
screen /skriːn/
website /'websaɪt/

Verbs

access /'ækses/
crash /kræʃ/
delete /dɪ'liːt/
download /ˌdaʊn'ləʊd/
print /prɪnt/
save /seɪv/
surf /sɜːf/

JOBS

Nouns

actor /'æktə/
architect /'ɑːkɪtekt/
artist /'ɑːtɪst/
butcher /'bʊtʃə/
cameraman /'kæmərəmæn/
career /kə'rɪə/
carpenter /'kɑːpəntə/
chef /ʃef/
chemist /'kemɪst/
cleaner /'kliːnə/
comedian /kə'miːdiən/
customs officer /'kʌstəmz
  'ɒfɪsə/
dancer /'dɑːntsə/
dentist /'dentɪst/
designer /dɪ'zaɪnə/
detective /dɪ'tektɪv/
disc jockey /dɪsk 'dʒɒki/
employment /ɪm'plɔɪmənt/
engineer /ˌendʒɪ'nɪə/
farmer /'fɑːmə/
film star /fɪlm stɑː/
fire fighter /faɪə 'faɪtə/
flight attendant /flaɪt
  ə'tendənt/
hairdresser /'heəˌdresə/
income /'ɪnkʌm/
journalist /'dʒɜːnəlɪst/
judge /dʒʌdʒ/
labourer /'leɪbərə/
lawyer /'lɔɪə/
librarian /laɪ'breəriən/
mechanic /mə'kænɪk/
musician /mjuː'zɪʃən/
newsagent /'njuːzˌeɪdʒənt/
novelist /'nɒvəlɪst/
nurse /nɜːs/
occupation /ˌɒkjʊ'peɪʃən/
pay /peɪ/
physician /fɪ'zɪʃən/
poet /'pəʊɪt/
police officer /pə'liːs 'ɒfɪsə/
porter /'pɔːtə/
profession /prə'feʃən/
publisher /'pʌblɪʃə/
salary /'sæləri/
sales assistant /seɪlz ə'sɪstənt/
security guard /sɪ'kjʊərɪti gɑːd/
singer /'sɪŋə/
trade /treɪd/
travel agent /trævəl 'eɪdʒənt/
TV presenter /tiː'viː prɪ'zentə/
wage /weɪdʒ/
waiter /'weɪtə/

Verbs/Verb phrases

deal with
look after
serve /sɜːv/

Adjectives

unskilled /ʌn'skɪld/

APPLYING FOR A JOB

Nouns

advertisement /əd'vɜːtɪsmənt/
application form /ˌæplɪ'keɪʃən
  fɔːm/
candidate /'kændɪdət/
experience /ɪk'spɪəriəns/
interview /'ɪntəvjuː/
job offer /dʒɒb 'ɒfə/
pay and conditions /peɪ ən
  kən'dɪʃənz/

Adjectives

full-time /ˌfʊl'taɪm/
hard-working /ˌhɑːd'wɜːkɪŋ/

Verbs/Verb phrases

accept /ək'sept/
attend /ə'tend/
discuss /dɪ'skʌs/
earn /ɜːn/
employ /ɪm'plɔɪ/
fill in
receive /rɪ'siːv/

BUSINESS AND INDUSTRY

Nouns

accounts department /ə'kaʊnts
  dɪ'pɑːtmənt/
appointment /ə'pɔɪntmənt/
assistant /ə'sɪstənt/
boss /bɒs/
brochures /'brəʊʃəz/
building /'bɪldɪŋ/
business /'bɪznɪs/
business trip /'bɪznɪs trɪp/
businessman /'bɪznɪsmən/
canteen /kæn'tiːn/
clerk /klɑːk/
colleague /'kɒliːg/
conference /'kɒnfərəns/
contract /'kɒntrækt/
customer /'kʌstəmə/
customer services /'kʌstəmə
  'sɜːvɪsɪz/
delivery /dɪ'lɪvəri/
department /dɪ'pɑːtmənt/
director /daɪ'rektə/
employer /ɪm'plɔɪə/
factory /'fæktəri/
machine /mə'ʃiːn/
manager /'mænɪdʒə/
meeting /'miːtɪŋ/
product /'prɒdʌkt/
project /'prɒdʒekt/
receptionist /rɪ'sepʃənɪst/
report /rɪ'pɔːt/

sales figures /seɪlz fɪɡəz/
secretary /'sekrətəri/
staff /stɑːf/
suppliers /sə'plaɪəz/

Adjectives

in stock
on strike

Verbs

arrange /ə'reɪndʒ/
cancel /'kænsəl/
confirm /kən'fɜːm/
deliver /dɪ'lɪvə/
insure /ɪn'ʃʊə/
manage /'mænɪdʒ/
meet /miːt/
operate /'ɒpəreɪt/
order /'ɔːdə/
retire /rɪ'taɪə/
run /rʌn/
sign /saɪn/
type /taɪp/